DISCOVER DARK PSYCHOLOGY

How to read People Through Body Language. Learn the Darkest Techniques of Manipulation and Persecution, How to Use Them and How to Defend Yourself from Them

By

Jake Bishops

Table of Contents

Introduction 16

How Dark Psychology Is Used Today? 17
Dark Psychology Tactics That Are Used regularly .. 18
   Love Flooding 18
   Lying 18
   Love Denial 19
   Withdrawal 19
   Restricting Choices 19
   Semantic Manipulation 19
   Reverse Psychology 20
Who Will Deliberately Use Dark Tactics? 20
   Narcissists 20
   Sociopaths 21
   Politicians 21
   Salespeople 21
   Leaders 22
   Selfish People 22
Wide, Practical and Theoretical Observations 23
The Code of Hammurabi 24

Chapter 1: The Art of Persuasion - NLP 27

- Which Side of the Brain Their Subject Uses? 31
- Which Sense Is Most Important to Them? 32
- How Their Brain Stores Information 32
- When They Are Lying or Making Things Up. 33
- How to Make Someone Drop Their Guard 34
- How You Can Condition People Without Their Consent/Knowledge 34
- Listen and Watch 35
- Building Rapport with Others.................................. 36

Chapter 2: Body Language 38

- Lower Body 40
- Legs Touching 40
- Pointing Feet 41
- Smarty Pants 41
- Shy Tangle 42
- Upper Body 42
- Leaning 42
- The Superman 43
- The Chest in Profile 44
- Outward Thrust Chest 44
- Hands 44

Control 45

Greeting 46

Dominance 46

Affection 46

Submission 47

Holding 47

Chapter 3: Mind Control Techniques 50

Recognizing the Art of Manipulation 51

Persuasive Language 52

Techniques Used in Mind Control 53

Chapter 4: Stop the Manipulators 59

Chapter 5: Persuasion and Influence 69

The Six Weapons of Persuasion 71

Reciprocity 71

Commitment and Consistency 72

Social Proof 73

Chapter 6: Psychology and Dark NLP 78

Personality Does Not Go Away 81

What You Need to Know 84

Play on Hope and Fear 86

Insult Someone Subtly 87

Chapter 7: Thoughts and Actions 89

Link between Thoughts, Decisions, Actions, and

Results 89
   Thoughts 90
   Feelings 91
   Behaviors 91

Chapter 8: What is Emotional Manipulation? 97

Specific Types of Emotional Manipulation 98
   Lying 99
   Lying by Omission 99
   Denial 99
   Rationalization 99
   Minimization 100
   Selective Attention and/or Inattention 100
   Diversion 100
   Evasion 100
   Covert Intimidation 101
   Guilt-tripping 101
   Shaming 101
   Blaming the Victim 101
   Playing the Victim 102
   Playing the Servant 102
   Seduction 102
   Projection 103
   Feigning Innocence 103
   Feigning Confusion 103

Peer Pressure *104*

Signs That You're Being Manipulated 104

Specific Examples of Emotional Manipulation 106

Chapter 9: Dark Criminals among Us 111

Criminal Mind vs. Cybercriminal Mind 114

The Role of Psychology in the Legal System 114

The Roles of a Criminal Psychologist 116

   Clinical *116*

   Experimental *117*

   Advisory *117*

   Actuarial *118*

   Profiling *118*

Applied Criminal Psychology 121

Chapter 10: How the Mind Works When It Is Manipulated 123

Using Isolation to Get What You Want 124

Criticism 126

Alienating the Target to Get What They Want 129

Using Social Proof as a Form of Peer Pressure 131

Chapter 11: The Role of Defense 132

The Steps to Raise Self-Esteem 133

   Acceptance *133*

   Increase Awareness *136*

Detach with Love *138*

Chapter 12: Toxic People **142**

How Negative and Toxic People Affect Your Life . 148

Managing Negative Thoughts 148

Chapter 13: How to Fake Your Body Language **151**

Concentrate on the Eyes - Eye Conduct Can Be Telling 151

Look at the Face - Body Language Touching Mouth or Smiling 152

Focus on Vicinity 153

Check Whether the Other Individual Is Reflecting You 154

Take a Quick Check at the Other Individual's Feet 155

Watch for Hand Signals 156

Look at the Situation of the Arms 157

A Wrinkled Brow Can Occur in a Brief Instant and Uncover Negative Feelings 159

Chapter 14: Undetected Mind Control **163**

Undetected Mind Control Tactics 165

Finding Those Who Are in Need *165*

Media Control with Images *167*

Restricting Choice *169*

Media Mind Control with Sound *170*

Chapter 15: Effects of Narcissism in Relationships **173**

Why Am I Attracting Narcissists? 175
   Caregiving Spirit *177*
   You Fall for the Name-Dropping Charm *177*
   Flattery Is Your Undoing *178*
   Hovering for a Second Chance *179*
   You Sustain the Drama *180*
   You Are a Hopeless Empath *181*
   Why Empaths Attract Narcissists *182*
   You Are a Natural Healer *183*

Chapter 16: Brainwashing **184**

What Is Brainwashing? 184
Methods 185
Techniques That Are Used in Brainwashing 185
   Isolation *185*
   Chanting and Singing *186*
   Love Bombing *186*
   Barratrous Abuse *188*
   Fatigue and Sleep Deprivation *188*
   Activity Pedagogy *189*
   Lifton's Process *189*
   Assault on Identity *190*

Guilt *190*

Self-Betrayal *191*

Leniency *191*

Compulsion to Confession *191*

Challenging of Guilt *192*

Self-Rebuilding 193

Progress and Harmony *193*

Final Confession and Rebirth *193*

Chapter 17: Covert Hypnosis 195

Techniques 196

Covert Hypnosis and Media *198*

Covert Hypnosis in Fiction *198*

Learning Covert Hypnosis *199*

Get into the Right Learning Mind Frame *199*

Build Rapport *200*

Look for Trance Signals *200*

Understand Hypnotic Language 201

What Hypnosis Is and Is Not *202*

Advantages of Covert or Conversational Hypnosis *202*

Covert Hypnosis Is a Simple Way to Convince People *203*

Research-Based Evidence on Use and Utility *206*

Covert Hypnosis Explained *206*

Getting Ready for Covert Hypnosis 207

Chapter 18: How to Use Dark Psychology to Succeed at Work 208

Chapter 19: Knowing the Woman's Mind 217

How Women Process Attraction 219

Chapter 20: Characteristics of Manipulative People 224

How Manipulators Select Their Victims 226

Signs of a Manipulative Partner 228

How to Know You Are Being Targeted 230

How to Deal with a Manipulator 231

Chapter 21: Victims 235

Traits of a Victim 235

Empathetic 236

Caregiver 237

Codependent 238

Grew Up in Dysfunction 239

Low Self-Esteem 239

Signs of Abuse or Manipulation 241

Self-Sacrificing or Martyrdom 241

Self-Sabotage 241

Fiercely Protective of Abuser 242

Mental Health Issues 243

Being Distrustful *243*

Fearful Behavior *243*

Paranoia *244*

Chapter 22: Deception **245**

The Types of Deception 247

Lies *249*

Equivocations *249*

Concealments *249*

Exaggerations *250*

Understatements *250*

Untruthful *250*

Identity *251*

Relational *251*

Instrumental *251*

Simulation *252*

How to Use Deception 253

Chapter 23: Distance in Communication **255**

Chapter 24: When "No" Means "Yes" **264**

Chapter 25: Subliminal Persuasion **273**

Cold Reading 277

Conclusion **283**

© Copyright 2020 by Jake Bishops - All rights reserved.

This book is provided with the sole purpose of providing relevant information on a specific topic for which every reasonable effort has been made to ensure that it is both accurate and reasonable. Nevertheless, by purchasing this book, you consent to the fact that the author, as well as the publisher, are in no way experts on the topics contained herein, regardless of any claims as such that may be made within. As such, any suggestions or recommendations that are made within are done so purely for entertainment value. It is recommended that you always consult a professional before undertaking any of the advice or techniques discussed within.

This is a legally binding declaration that is considered both valid and fair by both the Committee of Publishers Association and the American Bar Association and should be considered as legally binding within the United States.

The reproduction, transmission, and duplication of any of the content found herein, including any specific or extended information, will be done as an illegal act regardless of the end form the information ultimately takes. This includes copied versions of the work, physical, digital, and audio unless express consent of the Publisher is provided beforehand. Any additional rights reserved.

Furthermore, the information that can be found within the pages described forthwith shall be considered both accurate and truthful when it comes to the recounting of facts. As such, any use, correct or incorrect, of the provided information will render the publisher free of responsibility as to the actions taken outside of their direct purview. Regardless, there are zero scenarios where the original author or the publisher can be deemed liable in any fashion for any damages or hardships that may result from any of the information discussed herein.

Additionally, the information in the following pages is intended only for informational purposes and should thus be thought of as universal. As befitting its nature, it is presented without assurance regarding its prolonged validity or interim quality. Trademarks that are mentioned are done without written consent and can in no way be considered an endorsement from the trademark holder.

Introduction

Psychology is going to underpin everything in our lives from advertising to finance, crime to religion, and even from hate to love. Someone who can understand these psychological principles is someone who holds onto the key to human influence.

This is not an easy task which is why most people don't possess it. Learning all the different principles of psychology is not necessary. Start with the lessons on these pages, and you'll have a solid foundation. You have to be able to read people, understand what makes them tick, and understand why they may react in ways that may not be normally expected. And even then, you may need to spend time taking classes and reading through countless books to gain a complete understanding. It depends on how far you want to go with this.

So, if only a few people understand psychology and how the human mind works, why is it so important to know what this is? It is because those who do know what it is and how to use it can choose to use that power and that knowledge against you.

How Dark Psychology Is Used Today?

While some people are going to use these dark psychology tactics to harm their victim, there are times when you may use these tactics without the intent of negatively manipulating another person. Some of these tactics were either unintentionally or intentionally added to our toolbox from a variety of means that could include:

When you were a child, you would see how adults, especially those close to you, behaved.

When you were a teenager, the mind and your ability to understand the behaviors around you were expanded truly.

You were able to watch others use the tactics and then succeed.

Using the tactics may have been unintentional in the beginning, but when you found that it worked to get you what you wanted, you would start to use those tactics intentionally.

Some people, such as a politician, a public speaker, or a salesperson, would be trained to use these types of tactics to get what they want.

Dark Psychology Tactics That Are Used regularly

Love Flooding

This would include any buttering up, praising, or complimenting people to get them to comply with the request that you want. If you want someone to help you move some items into your home, you may use love flooding to make them feel good, which could make it more likely that they will help you. A dark manipulator could also use it to make the other person feel attached to them and then get them to do things that they may not normally do.

Lying

This would include telling the victim an untrue version of the situation. It can also include a partial truth or exaggerations to get what you wanted to be done.

Love Denial

This one can be hard on the victim because it can make them feel lost and abandoned by the manipulator. This one includes withholding affection and love until you can get what you want out of the victim.

Withdrawal

This would be when the victim is given the silent treatment or is avoided until they meet the needs of the other person.

Restricting Choices

The manipulator may give their victim access to some choices, but they do this to distract them from the choices that they don't want the victim to make.

Semantic Manipulation

This is a technique where the manipulator is going to use some commonly known words, ones that have accepted meanings by both parties, in a conversation. But then they will tell the victim later on, that they had meant something completely different when they used that word. The new meaning is often going to change upthe entire definition and could make it so that the conversation goes the way the manipulator wanted, even though the victim was tricked.

Reverse Psychology

This is when you tell someone to do something in one manner, knowing that they will do the opposite. But the opposite action is what the manipulator wanted to happen in the first place.

Who Will Deliberately Use Dark Tactics?

Many different people may choose to use these dark tactics against you. They can be found in many different aspects of your life, which is why it is so important to learn how to stay away from them. Some of the people who can use some of these dark psychology tactics deliberately include:

Narcissists

These individuals are going to have a bloated sense of their self-worth, and they will need to make others believe that they are superior as well. To meet their desires of being worshipped and adored by everyone they meet, they will use persuasion and dark psychology.

Sociopaths

Those who are sociopaths are charming, intelligent, and persuasive. But they only act this way to get what they want. They lack any emotions. This means that they have no issue with using the tactics of dark psychology to get what they want, including taking it as far as creating superficial relationships.

Politicians

With the help of dark psychology, a politician could convince someone to cast votes for them simply by convincing these people that their point of view is the right one.

Salespeople

Not all salespeople are going to use dark tactics against you. But it is possible that some, especially those who are really into getting their sales numbers and being the best, will not think twice about using dark persuasion to manipulate people.

Leaders

Throughout history, there have been plenty of leaders who will use the techniques of dark psychology to get their team members, subordinates, and citizens to do what they want.

Selfish People

This could be any person that you come across who will make sure that their own needs are put before anyone else's. They aren't concerned about others, and they will let others forego their benefits so that they can benefit. If the situation benefits them, it is fine if it benefits someone else. But if someone is going to be the loser, it will be the other person and not them.

This list is important because it is going to serve two purposes. First, it is going to help you be more aware of the people who may try to manipulate you to do things that you don't want to do, and it can be there to help out with self-realization.

Wide, Practical and Theoretical Observations

Murder, rape, incest, abuse, all words that can send chills up your spine. As a culture, we have saturated ourselves with negative ideals for entertainment purposes. We sit and watch horror movies, crime shows, and reality shows diving into the minds of the deviant. The darkness within these becomes an obsession for some, and though they don't reenact or find the actions preferable, there is a connection that few want to recognize outwardly. While the majority of human beings have a buffer in their mind, knowing fact from fiction and right from wrong, some lack it.

Imagination is one thing. Combing through the worst fears of people to find what scenario can be the scariest and most grabbing is something that fiction writers and creators do. Often though, when watching these dark psyches at work on the screen in front of you, the human mind finds certain recognition of why the predator or villain did what they did. Some movies and books even prey on the idea of the worst human condition. Depraved and distraught, the father who witnessed his family's murders climbs out of his ominous depression to wreak havoc on those that committed the acts to begin with. There is a satisfaction for people in therevenge of heinous acts. But then, doesn't that apply thesame dark psyche to the perpetrator, regardless of the reasoning behind it?

Dark Psychology has no pointed targets and cares little for the reasoning behind the actions. It is the actual act of manipulation, deceit, and harm that carries the weight within the dark psyche. The idea of revenge has been around a very long time, and at some significant points in history was considered a requirement of honor if the wrong was done to you. Very clear examples of the "eye for an eye" concept are still in existence today. The death penalty is one such example, though the root of it is wide and doesn't currently encourage private actions of one person to another. The federal organization as a whole is in charge of carrying out the punishment. But long before that, laws were erected in civilizations that based themselves on the idea of revenge.

The Code of Hammurabi

The Code of Hammurabi dates back to Babylonian times. Around 1760 B.C., the king of Babylon set forth a stone pillar inscribed with the laws of his kingdom. They are considered the oldest discovered set of laws in our history as human beings. What is so significant about the Code of Hammurabi? It is the fact that it is set in the pure idea of revenge. King Hammurabi believed wholeheartedly in the idea of an eye for an eye and set forth over thirty laws of Babylon based on that specific theory.

Through time, this code has shown its influence through almost all judicial and legal systems. Even the American justice system is predicated on the idea of an eye for an eye. A punishment system where retribution for a crime is equal in severity to the crime committed. What was not expected or understood was the fact that this revenge system is actually internally governed by a specific part of our brains called the dorsal striatum. This sector controls the idea of revenge within our minds. For victims of crime, the dorsal striatum is more active. So ultimately, with a society of an eye for an eye, we are taking the actions of a dark psyche and melding a new one from their actions.

One very prominent case of revenge on a large scale would be the St. Bartholomew's Day Massacre. This massacre occurred during the Protestant Reformation in the sixteenth century. During this time, a new sect of Christianity had been created, and the Catholic Church stood to lose control and power over people, land, and money. In August 1572, the French Protestants flooded Paris for the marriage of a Catholic woman to a Protestant aristocrat. When the wedding was over, King Charles IX ordered that the aristocrat be killed for his crimes to the church. To make it as easy as possible, he also ordered the murder of the Protestants within the town and then outward into the French countryside. That case of revenge cost society between thousand and four thousand lives.

Chapter 1: The Art of Persuasion - NLP

Perhaps you were considering being hypnotized yourself and you wanted to know more about the process. Or maybe you have always considered a career in psychology, in particular, hypnotherapy.

Many people wonder if hypnosis can be used to persuade people—to win arguments, negotiate purchases and sell people things, and so on. The truth is that hypnosis truly is meant to be a therapy. That is, the field of hypnosis originated with psychologists whose goal was to help people change undesirable attitudes, fears, and behaviors. With hypnotherapy, a therapist can delve deep into a person's subconscious and reprogram how that person thinks and reacts in their waking state.

Yet there are other ways to use the subconscious.

Hypnotherapy uses several different techniques. Among these are the ideas of mirroring and leading, strategies that are part of another area of psychological study called neuro-linguistic programming, or NLP, as it is commonly called. NLP is a method of changing how we communicate with others to create more favorable outcomes for ourselves and those we communicate with. That is, if you understand NLP you better understand how people think and behave, and you better understand how to have productive interactions with people—interactions that accomplish goals, both yours and theirs.

We will talk briefly about NLP, teaching you a few concepts that you can use in your everyday life to have more beneficial interactions with other people. You can also use these tips if you go into hypnosis practice to build a better rapport with your subjects and to best help them achieve their goals.

NLP is a way of reading body language and mood and using this information to lead the other person where you want them to go. When you properly implement NLP, you can communicate better with your partner, be a better parent, work better with your colleagues, communicate more effectively with your boss, and more. When you learn NLP, you learn to know yourself better, to read what other people are thinking, and to have a direct impact on the world.

Psychologists and laypeople have used the practice of NLP for decades. Somewhat similar to hypnosis, NLP is both an art and a science, an idea that is founded on sound observation and research, yet a skill that is developed through practice and mindfulness. Put simply, NLP is a type of subconscious programming (just like hypnosis!); it's something that we all exhibit every day. For example, if someone says something that upsets you, you may subconsciously tighten your jaw and your body muscles, staying very still as you process the information. This is a subconscious response, part of our fight-or-flight tendencies, which first tell your body to freeze as you access a situation.

Many therapists use NLP techniques in counseling their clients, as NLP can be a very effective way to manage phobias and anxiety. NLP counseling can also help people who have had a difficult past (perhaps with abuse or trauma) to move on and learn to manage their memories. NLP has been used by dating coaches to help instill confidence in their clients and by marketing professionals to better reach their target markets. NLP can also be used on one's self in a very simple way but with profound outcomes. Let's look at a few of the most fundamental NLP concepts, and how you can use this subconscious programming to benefit you and others in everyday life.

NLP has been used in alternative medicine to treat illnesses like Parkinson's disease. It has also been used in psychotherapy, advertisement, sales, management, coaching, teaching, team building, and public speaking. Yes, each one of these categories is a form of manipulation to some degree. You can't go to a class, the grocery store, or even a restaurant without being subject to some form of manipulation. No matter where you are, you can't escape it. It's present in advertisement posters, the tactic of that business sales clerk that stopsyou at the mall, the product placement in the movie you're watching, and everywhere else. However, instead of being afraid of this knowledge, you can use it to your advantage and redirect that manipulation as the wielder.

But some skilled individuals can harness this power to give them an unbeatable advantage. The techniques are best used in a one-on-one or small group environment.

The fewer people involved, the easier it is to read and apply NLP methods.

NLP is a complex subject and is often taught over years. That's because it takes practice to learn the range of reactions people can express. But the promise of learning people's inner secrets makes this technique especially attractive to con artists and law enforcement.

A skilled NLP user can determine:

Which Side of the Brain Their Subject Uses?

People fall along a spectrum between creative and analytical. New science shows that brain function is distributed across the brain. But it is still helpful to think of people through this lens.

Word choice, sentence structure, and associations all reveal details about the person that uses them. Left-brained people often use words that elicit emotions or experiences. Right-brained people like to include things outside their experience or expertise.

Which Sense Is Most Important to Them?

We have more than the five senses (sight, sound, taste, touch, and smell) most people know about. We also have a sense of order, balance, morality, and a host of others, and each of us has one or two that are more important than the rest.

How Their Brain Stores Information

Our brains are the most complex computers we have ever come across. They store and process billions of bits of information for a second. Each one functions a little differently. One of the biggest areas of divergence is in how people store information.

Some individuals have a memory like a sponge, soaking up everything near them. Others are more like a filter that catches big chunks and allows everything to pass through. NLP techniques help people discern the difference and to what degree.

Over time, NLP users get better at keeping track of information. With enough time, users can improve their information tracking abilities to near-genius levels. This gives us an advantage over anyone who isn't as experienced or naturally gifted.

When They Are Lying or Making Things Up.

People perform specific behaviors when they make things up called "tells." NLP users like me can pick up on these tells and be able to call out the liar as they lie. Some people are better than others at lying, but everyone has at least one tell.

Skilled liars understand that for someone else to believe their lie, so must they. So they convince themselves of it first. They often don't display all the signs of dishonesty because they truly believe the lie as they tell it.

Practice can help people fall for their lies, but the process demands a selective memory. This feature is more reliably detected than the oft-cited slight downward glance. It also proves to be a more consistent indicator of ingrained deception than awkward looks.

Power imbalances also make a refusal to make eye contact less reliable as well.

How to Make Someone Drop Their Guard

When someone likes you, they want to include you in their lives. Listening to what they say often provides deep insight into what controls their lives. People offer up their darkest secrets willingly, believing that I truly understand them.

How You Can Condition People Without Their Consent/Knowledge

Let's face it; people don't like finding out someone was manipulating them. It violates the idea that we are in control of our lives. But sometimes the truth is hard to take, and we need someone to help us see the way without calling us out on it.

We all manipulate those around us to one degree or another. This can be as simple as breaking a bad habit or establishing new relationship rules with a toxic family member. By steering them in the right direction, we can help them respond to how we prefer.

NLP doesn't brainwash someone (that's covered elsewhere) or cause them to do something out of character. But it does reveal the strings that control each of us. What you do with those strings once you have them is up to you.

Listen and Watch

This is the most time-consuming step, as it is the basis of building the structure for the more intimate relationship you'll build later. Body language is essential to NLP practices. Not only is it vital to the beginning, but knowing how to read body language comes into play throughout the NLP process and any other psychological process. Luckily, the longer you build a relationship with someone, the easier it will be to know they tell, as they are developed from habit. Some people may be guarded around you, which will appear as tense or straight shoulders and back, notholding your gaze, or even fidgeting. This is a sign you aren't building a vital rapport. Before moving any further, this person needs to feel relaxed and warm around you. Watch for an open face, a relaxed smile, and some easy-going interaction such as light laughter. Stay away from heavy topics until this person is comfortable with you.

Building Rapport with Others

Every day we use our communications to try and influence others. Unfortunately, most of us are rarely successful because we don't know what we are doing—we don't understand the psychology of other people. We don't know how to get into another person's subconscious mind.

One important aspect of getting on well with others is the building of rapport. First, let's consider what rapport is. Rapport is simple, it is the magic that happens when two people are getting along really well and communicating on the same level. When you have a rapport with another person, you are each understanding the other; you are listening better, and you are accomplishing something.

You do not have to think the same way as another person or agree with everything they say to have rapport. You simply have to be communicating similarly. One way that people show rapport is when they mirror each other, that is to say, they have similar body language. People who have a good rapport use similar body language, including posture and eye contact. Imagine in your head that you are talking and laughing with a friend. Likely, you are both standing with your feet a comfortable width apart, your arms moving animatedly as you speak, you are both smiling, and your eyes make frequent contact.

Chapter 2: Body Language

Being able to communicate well is extremely important when wanting to succeed in the personal and professional world, but it isn't the words you say that scream. It is your body language that does the screaming. Your gestures, posture, eye contact, facial expressions, and tone of voice are your best communication tools. These can confuse, undermine, offend, build trust, draw others in, or put someone at ease.

There are many times where what someone says and what their body language says is different. Non-verbal communication could do five things:

- **Substitute** – It could be used in place of a verbal message.
- **Accent** – It could underline or accent your verbal message.
- **Complement** – It could complement or add to what you are saying verbally.

- **Repeat** – It could strengthen and repeat your verbal message.
- **Contradict** – It could go against what you are trying to say verbally to make your listener think that you are lying.

We are going to cover:

- **Gestures** – These have been woven into our lives. You might speak animatedly; argue with your hands, point, wave, or beckon. Gestures do change according to cultures.
- **Facial expressions** – You will learn that the face is expressive and able to show several emotions without speaking one word. Unlike what you say and other types of body language, facial expressions are usually universal.
- **Eye contact** – Because sight tends to be our strongest sense for most people, it is an important part of Non-verbal communication. The way someone looks at you could tell you whether they are attracted to you, affectionate, hostile, or interested. It might also help the conversation flow.

- **Body movement and posture** – Take a moment to think about how you view people based on how they hold their head, stand, walk around, and sit. The way people carry themselves gives you a lot of information. Non-verbal communication could go wrong in several different ways.

Lower Body

The arms share a lot of information. The hands share a lot more, but legs give us the exclamation point and can tell us exactly what someone is thinking. The legs could tell you if a person is open and comfortable. They could also who dominance or where they want to go.

Legs Touching

When a person is standing, they will only be able to touch their bottom or thighs. This can be done seductively or they could slap their legs as if they are saying "Let's go." It might also indicate irritation. This is when you have to pay attention to the context of the conversation. This is very important.

Pointing Feet

Look at the direction of a person's feet to see where their attention is. Their feet will always point toward what is on their mind or what they are concentrating on. Everyone has a lead foot, and it all depends on their dominant hand. If a person is talking that we are interested in is talking, our lead foot will be pointing toward them. But, if they want to leave the situation, you will notice their foot pointing toward an exit or the way they want to go. If a person is sitting during the conversation, look at where their feet are pointing to see what they are truly interested in.

Smarty Pants

This is a position where someone tries to make them look bigger. They will usually be seated with their legs splayed open and leaning back. They might even spread their arms out and lock them behind their head. This is normally used by people who feel dominant, superior, or confident.

Shy Tangle

This is usually something that women do more than men. Anyone who begins to feel shy or timid will sometimes entangle their legs by crossing them under and over to try to block out bad emotions and to make them look smaller. There is another shy leg twirl that people will do when they are standing. The actual act of this movement is crossing one leg over the other and hooking that foot behind their knee as if they are trying to scratch an itch.

Upper Body

Upper body language can show signs of defensiveness since the arms could easily be used as a shield. Upper body language could involve the chest. Let's look at some upper body language.

Leaning

If someone leans forward, it will move them closer to another person. There are two possible meanings to this. First, it will tell you that they are interested in something, which could just be what you are talking about. But this movement could also show romantic interest. Second, leaning forward could invade a person's personal space; hence, this shows them as a threat. This is often an aggressive display. This is done unconsciously by powerful people.

The Superman

Bodybuilders, models commonly use this, and it was made popular by Superman. This could have various meanings depending on how a person uses it. Within the animal world, animals will try to make themselves look bigger when they feel threatened. If you look at a house cat when they get spooked, they will stretch their legs and their fur stands on end. Humans also have this, even if it isn't as noticeable. This is why we get goosebumps. Because we can't make ourselves look bigger, we have to come up with arm gestures like putting our hands on our waist. This shows us that a person is getting ready to act assertively.

This is normal for athletes to do before a game or a wife who is nagging their spouse. A guy who is flirting with a girl will use this to look assertive. This is what we call a readiness gesture.

The Chest in Profile

If a person stands sideways or at a 45-degree angle, they are trying to accentuate their chest. They might also thrust out their chest, more on this in a minute. Women do this posture to show off their breasts, and men will do this to show off their profile.

Outward Thrust Chest

If someone pushes their chest out, they are trying to draw attention to this part of their body. This could also be used as a romantic display. Women understand that men have been programmed to be aroused by breasts. If you see a woman pushing her chest out, she might be inviting intimate relations. Men will thrust out their chest to show off their chest and possibly trying to hide their gut. The difference is that men will do this to women and other men.

Hands

Human hands have 27 bones and they are a very expressive part of the body. This gives us a lot of capability to handle our environment.

Reading palms isn't about just looking at the lines on the hands. After a person's face, the hands are the best source for body language. Hand gestures are different across cultures and one hand gesture might be innocent in one country but very offensive in another.

Hand signals may be small, but they show what our subconscious is thinking. A gesture might be exaggerated and done using both hands to show a point

Control

If a person is holding their hand with their palms facing down, they might be figuratively holding onto or restraining another person. This could be an authoritative action that is telling you to stop now. It might be a request asking you to calm down. This will be apparent if someone places their dominant hand on top of a handshake. If they are leaning on their desk withtheir palms flat, this shows dominance.

If their palms face outward toward another person, they might be trying to fend them off or push them away. They might be saying "stop, don't come closer."

If they are pointing their finger or their entire hand, they might be telling someone to leave now.

Greeting

Our hands are used a lot to greet other people. The most common way is with a handshake. Opening up the palm shows they don't have any weapons. This gets used when saluting, waving, or greeting others.

During this time, we get to touch another person and it might send various signals.

Dominance

It can be shown by shaking hands and placing the other hand on top. How long and how strong they shake the hand will tell you that they are deciding on when to stop the handshake.

Affection

It could be shown with the duration and speed of the handshake, smiles, and touching with the other hand. The similarity between this one and the dominant one could lead to a situation when a dominant person will try to pretend they are just being friendly.

Submission

It gets shown by placing their palms up. Floppy handshakes that are clammy along with a quick withdrawal also show submission.

Most handshakes use vertical palms that will show equality. They will be firm but won't crush and for the right amount of time so both parties know when they should let go.

Waving is a great way to greet people and could be performed from a long distance.

Salutes are normally done by the military, where a certain style is prescribed.

Holding

A person who has cupped hands shows they can hold something gently. They show delicacy or holding something fragile. Hands that grip will show desire, possessiveness, or ownership. The tighter the fist, the stronger they are feeling a specific emotion.

If someone is holding their own hands, they are trying to comfort themselves. They could be trying to restrain themselves so they will let somebody else talk. It could be used if they are angry and it is stopping them from attacking. If they are wringing their hands, they are feeling extremely nervous.

Holding their hands behind their back will show they are confident because they are opening up their front. They may hide their hands to conceal their tension. If one hand is gripping the other arm, the tighter and higher the grip, the tenser they are.

Two hands might show various desires. If one hand is forming a fist but the other is holding it back, this might show that they would like to punch somebody.

If someone is lying, they will try to control their hands. If they are holding them still, you might want to be a bit suspicious. Remember that these are just indicators and you should look for other signals.

If someone looks like they are holding onto an object like a pen or cup, this shows they are trying to comfort themselves. If a person is holding a cup but they are holding it very close and it looks like they are "hugging" the cup, they are hugging themselves. Holding onto any item with both hands shows they have closed themselves off from others.

Items might be used as a distraction to release nervous energy like holding a pen, but they are clicking it off and on, doodling, or messing with it. If their hands are clenched together in front of them but they are relaxed, and their thumbs are resting on each other, it might be showing pleasure.

Chapter 3: Mind Control Techniques

It's interesting to see that manipulation has been around for a long time, and that is not a new or imaginary concept. Understanding what the art of persuasion is all about is vital to help you to deal with it.

Here, we briefly look at the psychology of manipulation. This allows us to see where it might occur in our lives. It will also help you in identifying those who might attempt to manipulate you. It is not only about people who like to dominate. If we don't know it is happening to us, might be encouraged to act in ways that are incongruous to our normal personality and behavior. Learn how commerce can persuade customers into buying their goods and services. Recognizing such methods will help in dealing with the power of persuasion.

We like to believe that we are individuals who make sensible choices. In our journey of life, we do not always have full control, and we don't always realize this. As children, we are influenced by our parents and have little control over how we are raised. Once in the education system, we are further manipulated. The teachers will tell us all about the social norms and what is expected of us in society. As adults, we are lured in by politicians trying to get their share of votes. Many are persuaded to vote for a party because of what they promise for the future, even if they don't necessarily believe in their policies. This gives such politicians power, and their decisions will affect our lives. Are we in full control of our lives, or are we merely influenced by those who know all the tricks of persuasion?

We will look at how to deal with various manipulative methods, even sometimes covert. First, you need tolearn to recognize when you are being manipulated so you can counteract it.

Recognizing the Art ofManipulation

What then, in our everyday lives, do we need to be wary of?

Persuasive Language

The idiom that every picture tells a story is very true. Words can be so much more powerful as they inspire and encourage us, even to the point of manipulation. How many are the time you have been inspired by a good orator who's daring speech motives you into action? The art of words can be so influential in coercing us to believe something, even when our eyes tell us differently. Communication is a powerful tool, especially when it comes to making people do things.

Advertisers and salespeople use language to convince their goods are just what we are looking for. Using words, such as:

Affordable; Easy to use; Safe; Enjoyable; Time Saving; Guaranteed to last.

Note how all these words make us believe they are confident in their products.

Politicians will use language, such as:

- "We" to encompass you in their world.

- "Us" to make you feel a part of a team.

These are all communication tactics to make us feel included, therefore, important.

Bullies use language along with aggressive behavior to achieve their own selfish goals.

Criminal predators, such as psychopaths, sociopaths, and narcissists, are all people who learn the use of persuasive language. This is a means to get their way and gain control over another person.

Techniques Used in Mind Control

Present-day mind control is both innovative and mental. Tests demonstrate that basically by uncovering the techniques for mind control, the impacts can be diminished or disposed of, at any rate for mind control publicizing and promulgation. Increasingly hard to counter are the physical interruptions, which the military-mechanical complex keeps on creating and enhance.

1. Education — It has consistently been an eventual tyrant's definitive dream to "teach" normally receptive youngsters, subsequently, it has been a focal segment to

Communist and Fascist oppressive regimes from the beginning of time. Nobody has been increasingly instrumental in uncovering the motivation of present-day instruction than Charlotte Thompson Iserbyt—one can start an investigation into this region by downloading her book as a free PDF, *The Deliberate Dumbing Down of America*, revealing the job of Globalist establishments in forming a future planned to deliver servile automatons reigned over by a completely taught, mindful exclusive class.

2. Promotions and Propaganda – Edward Bernays has been referred to as the creator of the consumerist culture that was planned principally to focus on individuals' mental self-portrait (or scarcity in that department) to transform a need into a need. This was at first imagined for items, for example, cigarettes, for instance. Nonetheless, Bernays additionally noted in his 1928 book, Propaganda, that "purposeful publicity is the official arm of the imperceptible government." This can be seen most unmistakably in the advanced police state and the developing native nark culture, enveloped with the pseudo-enthusiastic War on Terror. The expanding union of media has empowered the whole corporate structure to converge with the government, which currently uses the idea of promulgation arrangement. Media; print, motion pictures, TV, and link news would now be able to work flawlessly to incorporate a general message which appears to have the ring of truth since it originates from such a significant number of sources at the same time. When one moves toward becoming sensitive to recognizing the fundamental "message," one will see this engraving all over. What's more, this isn't even to specify subliminal informing.

3. Prescient Programming – Many still deny that prescient computer writing programs are genuine. Prescient programming has its causes in predominately elitist Hollywood, where the big screen can offer a major vision of where society is going. For a nitty-gritty breakdown of explicit models, Vigilant Citizen is an incredible asset that will most likely make you take a gander at "amusement" in a unique light.

4. Sports, Politics, Religion – Some may resent seeing religion, or even legislative issues, put together with sports as a technique for mind control. The focal topic is the equivalent all through: isolate and prevail. The systems are very straightforward: impede the common propensity of individuals to participate for their endurance and train them to frame groups bowed on control and winning. Sports have consistently had a job as a key diversion that corrals innate propensities into a non-significant occasion, which in present-day America has arrived at silly extents where challenges will break out over a game VIP leaving their city. Yet, basic human issues, for example, freedom are chuckled away as immaterial.

5. Food, Water, and Air – Additives, poisons, and other nourishment harms modify mind science to make mildness and indifference. Fluoride in drinking water has been demonstrated to bring down IQ; Aspartame and MSG are excitotoxins which energize synapses until they kick the bucket; and simple access to the inexpensive food that contains these toxins, by and large, has made a populace that needs center and inspiration for a functioning way of life. The vast majority of the cutting-edge world is flawlessly prepped foruninvolved responsiveness—and acknowledgment—of the authoritarian tip top.

6. Medications — We can equate this to any addictive substance; however, the mission of mind controllers is to be certain you are dependent on something. One noteworthy arm of the cutting edge mind control motivation is psychiatry, which expects to characterize all individuals by their issue, instead of their human potential. Today, it has been taken to considerably assist limits as a medicinal oppression has grabbed hold where about everybody has a type of confusion—especially the individuals who question authority. The utilization of nerve tranquilizers in the military has prompted record quantities of suicides. To top it all off, the cutting edge medication state currently has over 25% of U.S. youngsters on mind-desensitizing drugs.

7. Military Testing — There is a long history associated with the military as the proving ground for mind control.

8. Electromagnetic Range — An electromagnetic soup encompasses all of us, charged by present-day gadgets of comfort which have been appeared to affect mind work directly. In an implicit affirmation of what is conceivable, one scientist has been working with a "divine being head protector" to instigate dreams by adjusting the electromagnetic field of the mind. Our advanced soup has us latently washed by conceivably mind-changing waves. At the same time, a wide scope of potential outcomes, for example, phone towers is currently accessible to the eventual personality controller for more straightforward mediation.

Mind control is more common than most people think. It is not easy to detect because of its subtle nature. In many instances, it happens under what is perceived as normal circumstances like through education, religion, TV programs, advertisements and so much more. Cults and their leadership use mind control to influence their members and control whatever they do. It is not easy to detect mind control. However, when one realizes it, they can get out and start again.

Chapter 4: Stop the Manipulators

Many manipulators will do their best to make sure that the victim doesn't realize what's happening, but there are ways to use this to your advantage.

By creating stakes, the manipulator has control over you because they know that either way they win. During those stakes, it's important to recognize that they don't expect you to not play their game.

A manipulator knows how to use dark psychology to make the victim do what they ask. If they are constantly picking on you or taking note of every mistake you've ever made, the manipulator is planning to use this against you. Their reactions to the things that disappoint them are important too.

Pay attention to how they respond to you in the beginning because this will change as time passes. The manipulator will take note of how you react to things not going your way. If you are prone to fits of rage yourself when frustrated, the manipulator will know how to use that against you. If you get depressed or are deeply saddened by failure, the manipulator will use that against you. Dark psychology focuses on human reaction to situations and using that to influence a situation.

A manipulator will focus on every reaction, every moment of joy, sadness, or anger, and twist it to suit their needs. For example, Liam and Cierra are brother and sister. Liam wants Cierra to stay home from summer camp this year because he doesn't want her to ruin his summer. Liam knows that Cierra doesn't like Sarah D. from her grade and would do anything to avoid her. Liam tells Cierra that this year Sarah is going to be at the summer camp and she's going to be bunking in her cabin. Cierra not wanting to spend a whole summer sleeping in the same room as Sarah drops out of the summer camp, and now Liam gets to go alone as he wanted. Something as simple as knowing that his sister didn't like another student was all he needed to manipulate her into doing what he wanted.

It's easy to manipulate someone into doing what you ask when you know what grinds their gears. Using dark psychology could make it easier for a manipulator to take advantage, and the victim wouldn't know how they allowed them to use these weaknesses.

Narcissistically, they would believe they are smarter than their victim and pay close attention to how they react to even the manipulator themselves. Manipulators love over-sharers or people who don't care who knows about their lives. These people are easier to manipulate because they lay everything about them on the table.

For example, Tyra is always talking about her bad marriage to John, John's friend that wants to have sex with Tyra knows how bad his marriage to his wife is and knows how John acts. Hence, he portrays the exact opposite of that and manipulates Tyra into sleepingwith him by complaining about his friendship with John.

A manipulator will always make things go their way by using keywords that may trigger a response out of the victim. They may berate them constantly for something small or make them feel guilty for having any reaction to what's happening around them at all. A manipulator's main tool to anything is pulling the wool over the victim's eyes. Dark persuasion is making the victim feel like they have no control over the situation or giving all the "power" to the victim. Prolonging events or constant empty promises may occur.

The manipulator will always show that they are in complete control, but it's up to the victim to say they aren't falling for it. They will find ways to make it feel like the victim has the power of choice, but the manipulator has carefully thought out every step from the moment they picked their victim.

Dark persuasion considers age, creed, upbringing, religion, and/or sexuality. The manipulator will take all these factors and create a trap for their victim. The victim would be completely unaware of what's happening, but they will feel like the events are correlated with their behavior or with what's happening as the situation transpires.

They won't be able to see how the manipulator has taken control of what's happening and leads them to do what they ask of them without much question. The manipulator is skilled at masking their true intentions of what they are doing, and the victim won't see they are being manipulated.

For example, Marie wants Donny to pay for her to go to Miami. She knows that Donny never got to travel because of his parents not being able to afford it, so she makes him feel bad that she can't afford it. Donny doesn't realize that she is doing this just to get her way and agrees to pay for the trip. Marie has known Donny for a few months and knew that from conversations they had together that something like that would work.

When unmasking the true intentions of another person, you must consider the person that you are dealing with. Sometimes you feel like they are manipulating the situation and when you feel that way, it's good to step up. However, if you can't identify the manipulation, one way is to focus on the person's choice of words.

If they are constantly repeating something or constantly return to one specific phrase in a spiral during a conflict, they are concentrating the focus on what they want. Look out for how they react to simple requests, something simple can become a chore for someone that is trying to manipulate a situation and they will use these repeated words or actions to get a rise of out the victim.

For example, Duncan doesn't want to do the dishes, so he complains to his sister about how he must do dishes all the time at work and that he gets cuts on his hands whenever he does them from the silverware and cutlery. Every time he doesn't want to do dishes, this is what Duncan will say and his sister will do it because she doesn't want her brother to suffer.

However, once she noticed that he only does this when he must do them, she eventually told him that she is no longer doing it. Once you recognize that you are being manipulated, it's easier to prevent it from continuing.

Manipulators may also get angry over very little things, to make themselves look and feel bigger. They will start fights over someone not listening to them or they will start a fight over the way a person looks at them.

A manipulator will shout, especially when they know they are in the wrong and don't want to admit it. As mentioned, if they feel cornered or don't know how to make themselves look like the victim, shouting is the next method. If someone for no reason just explodes, the fear they incite can make someone do what they want.

For example, Lorne wants Greg to stop asking him about why he came home late from work. Greg accuses him of cheating, Lorne tosses his coat down onto the floor and starts shouting at Greg for yelling at him whenhe's tired and has been working. Greg backs down because he is afraid of what would happen if he continued to yell at Lorne. And Lorne knew that Greg would if he yelled at him because Greg came from an abusive household. By knowing that piece and information and knowing his husband's reactions, Lorne can manipulate Greg and get what he wants.

It's these small interactions that manipulators need most, so pay close attention to how many questions they ask about your life. And pay attention to how much they share with you after they get the answers they want.

A manipulator would be hyper curious about your life or your friends or family. The victim would voluntarily share this with a boyfriend/girlfriend/partner, maybe even a close friend. If the manipulator seems to provide nothing to contribute to the stream of information they get, be careful with what is shared.

For example, Tammy knows everything about Veronika's life, but Veronika knows nothing about hers.

Tammy would always ask her best friend to talk about her life, but Veronika would provide little to nothing in retort. It's important to pay close attention to that information as well.

It could be basic, easily relatable topics to avoid talking about their real life and intentions. Or they could even set up for manipulation in the future by planting false stories about their lives into the conversation.

Manipulators will make sure that the victim is dependent purely on them, constantly creating a situation where they would be the higher authority and not be able to lose the rank they have over the victim. Taking them out of their comfort zone would be the most important part.

They would never let them go to a place where the victim could be superior.

For example, Frank doesn't want to go with Amy to her favorite diner. Frank prefers his diner because he's the important one and they care more about him than they would his date. He also wants Amy to think he's better than what she believes he is. Frank talks up the diner and convinces Amy to go with him to the diner. Being in that diner, Amy hears stories about Frank's childhood and learns only about the parts of his life that Frank wants her to know. A manipulator will censor the content that is available to you and make it impossible for you to look past the manipulation.

Censoring what you know can also come in the form of overusing information. A manipulator will spend more time correcting you. They will question your intelligence and won't believe you if you claim to know any information. To the manipulator, the victim is always wrong and doesn't know anything.

They will do whatever they can to make sure the only information the victim ever receives comes from them. Pay attention to how much they correct the small things you do; watch the number of times this occurs andwatch how they do it.

A manipulator might prevent them from going online or checking their phones or would get mad at them for trying to source check any information they come across during the relationship.

For example, Tom is with Jane. Tom doesn't want Jane to know anything about his past and gets angry with her every time she tries to look up anything. Tom deleted all photos on his social media accounts that had any inkling of him having any former partners as well as his old drug use. Tom doesn't want Jane to see anything beforeshe started seeing him, and when she asks about his past, Tom tells Jane he was a good student and didn't get into any trouble.

Chapter 5: Persuasion and Influence

There are many times when the human mind is pretty easy to influence, but it does take a certain set of skills to get people to stop and listen to you. Not everyone is good with influence and persuasion, though. They can talk all day and would not be able to convince others to do what they want. On the other hand, some could persuade anyone to do what they want, even if they had just met this person for the first time. Knowing how to work with these skills will make it easier for you to recognize a manipulator and be better prepared to avoid them if needed.

The first thing that we need to look at is what persuasion is. Persuasion is simply the process or action taken by a person or a group of people when they want to cause something to change. This could be with another human being and something that changes in their inner mental systems or their external behavior patterns.

The act of persuasion, when it is done properly, can sometimes create something new within the person, or it can just modify something already present in their minds. Three different parts come with the process of persuasion including:

- The communicator or other source of the persuasion.
- The persuasive nature of the appeal.
- The audience or the target person of the appeal.

All three elements must be taken into consideration before you try to do any form of persuasion on your own. You can just look around at the people who are in your life, and you will probably be able to see some types of persuasion happening all over the place.

The above options are all positive ways that you can use persuasion to your advantage. Most people will be amenable to these happening. But on the other side, there are four negative tactics of persuasion that you can do as well. These would include options like manipulating, avoiding, intimidating, and threatening. These negative tactics will be easier for the target to recognize, which is why most manipulators will avoid using them if possible.

Now, you can use some of the tactics above. Still, according to psychologist Robert Cialdini, six major principles of persuasion can help you to get the results that you want without the target being able to notice what is going on. Let us take a look at these six weapons and how they can be effective.

The Six Weapons of Persuasion

Reciprocity

The first principle of persuasion that you can use is known as reciprocity. This is based on the idea that when you offer something to someone, they will feel a bit indebted to you and will want to reciprocate it back. Humans are wired to be this way to survive. For the manipulator to use this option, they will make sure that they are doing some kind of favor for their target. Whether that is paying them some compliments, giving them a ride to work, helping out with a big project, or getting them out of trouble. Once the favor is done, the target will feel like they owe a debt to the manipulator. The manipulator will then be able to ask for something, and it will be really hard for the target to say no.

Commitment and Consistency

It is like humans to settle for what is already tried and tested in the mind. Most of us have a mental image of who we are and how things should be. And most people are not going to be willing to experiment, so they will keep on acting the way that they did in the past. So, to get them to work with this principle and do what you want, you first need to get them to commit to something. The steps that you would need to follow to get your target to do what you want through commitment and consistency include:

- Start out with something small. You can ask the target to do something small, something that is easier to manage the change before they start to integrate it more into their personality and get hooked on the habit.
- You can get the target to accept something publicly so that they will feel more obligated to see it through.
- Reward the target when they can stick to the course. Rewards will be able to help strengthen the interest of the target in the course of action that you want them to do.

Social Proof

This is another one that will rely on the human tendency, and it relies on the fact that people place a lot of value and trust in other people and in their opinions on things that we have not tried yet. This can be truer if the information comes from a close friend or a person who is perceived as the expert. It is impossible to try out everything in life and having to rely on others can put us at a disadvantage. This means that we need to find a reliable source to help us get started. A manipulator may be able to get someone to do something by acting as a close friend or an expert. They can get the target to try out a course of action because they have positioned themselves as the one who knows the most about the situation or the action.

Influence is a powerful, but often a subtle tool. The ability to affect or change someone's opinion, or create a change in circumstances without forcing the change directly is an art form all its own. Creating changes or conditions as situations develop creates a lasting impact. It can make others sit up and take notice of you and your presence and often create a perception of you that may make others want to defer to you in the future.

We will go over how to create influence, how to build your skills concerning influencing others, and how to utilize the influence you have built to achieve your goals.

Influence is based on basic, but key factors. Let's start with a room full of people whom you do not know. Your entrance into this room is vital. You may not know anyone, but not everyone present will know this. Presenting yourself in the most flattering way within the first few seconds will often dictate the way everyone in the room sees you. Smile as you enter the room, walking with your back and head in straight but relaxed alignment. Taking time not to rush or enter too slowly, imagine you are just walking into a room in your home. An often-effective trick to make you seem more approachable is to give a short wave as if you are acknowledging someone you know. This makes others assume that someone else in the room already knows you and that in and of itself makes you seem more likable or interesting.

When first meeting someone, making eye contact and firmly shaking their hand while smiling boosts your effective charisma with the other individual. Charisma is more about how you make the other person feel when they are in your presence. Charisma is not necessarily about being the life of the party. To work on your charisma; first, consider your own strengths. Are you humorous? Are you already outgoing and friendly? Do you tend to be shy and quieter? You can use any of your strengths to your advantage; it is all about understanding how to use them. If you are more of an introvert, pick one or two people off to the side of the crowd or room to engage with. When initiating communication, use your quieter presence to let others do more of the talking, and only steer the conversation in the direction you want it to go in when necessary. People love to talk about themselves! If you are outgoing, place yourself in a position of power, feel free to approach larger groupings of people, and greet them. Again, use your strengths to your advantage.

People that hold sway over others can attest, influence is all about give and take. When people feel a relationship is based on reciprocation, they trust the relationship easier and sooner and have fewer reservations. Try asking a small favor of someone, and then, in turn, offering them the same in return. An example would be offering to hold someone's place in line while they use the restroom, taking notes for them while they excuse themselves momentarily during a meeting or presentation, and then asking them to do the same for you upon their return. This 'give and take' lays a foundation of comradery, like you and the other party is already friendly. And people that feel like you like them, like you in return.

Building relationships overnight is not easy, but it can be easier by being friendly. Smiling and eye contact play a role in how you make other people feel. If you project that you are happy to see others that you are happy to be speaking with them, they will, in turn, feel happy to be communicating with you. Your body language speaks volumes, and others pick up on what you are conveying with yours, even if they aren't fully aware of it. When engaging with another, take note of how they are standing or sitting. If they are standing with their arms at their sides, you should mimic their stance. Mimicking someone's body language is another way of building an unspoken but solid foundation. If they are clearly exhibiting stress, mimic their stance. An example of this would be if their arms are crossed over the front of their body in a defensive pose. After a few minutes of conversation, move your arms to a more relaxed and natural position. In most instances, the person you are communicating with will subconsciously reposition their body language to mimic your own. This is an example of how you are already gaining influence and trust with someone you barely know.

When talking to individuals you want to gain influence over, another aspect to consider is your own attitude towards them. We know that our physical body language plays a role, and that reciprocating is important as well, but just as important is how you project yourself. Greeting another with a smile is great, but now that the conversation has started, maintains a neutral but relaxed facial expression. Staying involved and being attentive when others speak again makesthem feel good speaking with you. Asking questions per the flow of conversation shows that you are listening to them, and everyone wants to be heard. Being respectful,calm, and diplomatic in your interactions makes you more friendly and approachable. Showing gratitude for their time and being appreciated will encourage others to appreciate your attention and time in return.

Chapter 6: Psychology and Dark NLP

One of the many fundamental lessons of the Enneagram is that psychological incorporation and spiritual recognition are not different steps. Away from our spirituality, recognize that psychology might not relieve us or direct us to the inmost realities about ourselves, and with no psychology, spirituality can head to grandiosity, misconception, and an effort to escape from real life.

The Enneagram is not dry psychology, neither fuzzy mysticism nor an instrument for improvement that employs the clearness and perceptiveness of psychology as a point of entry into a deep and common spirituality. Therefore, in an actual sense, the Enneagram is "the link between psychology and spirituality."

The foremost of this hallowed psychology is that our fundamental type discloses the psychological mechanisms by which we overlook our real nature—our divine essence—the ways in which we leave ourselves.

Our personalities draw on the capabilities of our ingrained temperament to build resistance and compensations for where we've been harmed in early childhood. In an effort to endure no matter what difficulties, we all experienced during those times, we unknowingly figured out a limited collection of techniques, self-images, and habits that enabled us to deal with and thrive within our early environment. Every person consequently has become an "expert" at a certain type of coping which, when used overly, also gets to become the core of the dysfunctional aspect of our personality. As the barriers and methods of our personality get more organized, they cause us a loss of nearness to our direct experience of ourselves, our essence.

The personality ends up becoming the origin of our identity instead of contact with our being. Our experience of ourselves depends more and more on internal images, thoughts, as well as practiced behaviors instead of on the natural expression of our real nature. This loss of nearness to our essence leads to deep stress and anxiety, using the model of one of the nine passions. Once established, these passions, which happen to be commonly unconscious as well as hidden to us, start to drive the personality. Knowing our personality type, as well as its dynamics, accordingly offers a specifically potent strategy to the unconscious, to your pains and compensations, and eventually, to our recovery and improvement.

The Enneagram lets us see where our personality most "trips us up." It stresses simultaneously what's feasible for us, and how self-defeating and needless a lot of our old responses and conduct are. This is precisely why, when we finally identify with the personality, we're settling on becoming far less than who we are. It's like we had been offered a mansion to reside in, with luxurious furniture and beautifully kept grounds, but have restricted our-self within a smaller dark closet within the basement. Nearly all of us have even ignored that the other parts of the mansion are obtainable, or that we're actually its possessor. As spiritual instructors from the centuries have remarked, we've fallen asleep to ourselves and also to our personal lives. Much of the time, we walk around obsessed with ideas, worries, uncertainties, as well as mental images. Hardly ever are we present to ourselves and also to our immediate experience.

While we continue to fix ourselves, conversely, we start to see that our focus has been exploited or "magnetized" by the preoccupations and attributes of our personality and that we are in fact sleepwalking through most of life. This particular view of things is as opposed to common sense and frequently feels insulting to the manner by which we see ourselves—as self-determining, mindful, and in command. Simultaneously, our personality is not "bad." Our personality is an integral part of our development and is particularly essential for the refinement of our fundamental nature.

The issue is that we end up being stuck in personality and don't understand how to continue to the next stage. This isn't the outcome of any inherent flaw in us; instead, it's arrested development, which happens simply because almost no one in our developmental years was conscious that a lot was possible. Our parents as well as instructors perhaps have had some glimmers of their real nature; but like us, they usually did not identify them, much less live as expressions of them.

Personality Does Not Go Away

The objective of the Enneagram is merely not to allow us to remove our personality. In case we could manage to, it won't be very useful. This is comforting to those individuals who worry that if we get rid of our personality, we'll lose our identity or perhaps become less competent or efficient. In fact, exactly the opposite is true. Once we make contact with our essence, we do not lose our personality. It becomes more transparent and flexible, something that helps us live rather than something that takes over our lives. We are most existing and alert—attributes of essence—while the manifestations of our personality oftentimes cause us to disregard issues, make a few mistakes, and make dilemmas of all sorts.

NLP, neuro-linguistic programming, is a fascinating approach to persuasion and communication that works. Invented by Bandler and Grinder in the 1970s, NLP has since developed into a multi-billion-dollar industry that many people turn to for guidance. The methods taught by NLP help people learn how to banish bad memories, improve their cognition and mood, and learn to cope with mental issues, and even seduce or communicate better with other people.

The great thing about dark NLP is that it is applicable to all areas of life. You can use it for seduction, persuasion, deception, or even making yourself more confident and powerful. You can use it in romance, friendship, career, or family. You are invincible in all areas of your life when you start to use dark NLP.

NLP is built on the premise that you create the world around you. The way that the world appears to you is created through information filtered through your five senses, your speech patterns, and thought patterns taught to you when you were little. Some of your behavior is very unhelpful, but you can use NLP techniques to change this behavior and develop healthier habits.

You can use visualization, meditation, and even hypnosis on yourself to correct your maladaptive behavior habits. You can basically get into your own head and change your basic thought habits. NLP allows you to restructure your thinking and erase bad memories using your senses, language, and self-talk.

But based on this logic, you can also use NLP to enter the minds of others and restructure their thinking. And this is exactly what dark NLP entails. Dark NLP takes helpful NLP practices and flips them on other people. Dark NLP can be used for good or evil. Either way, it gives you significant control over others by allowing you to rewire their brains and affect their thinking.

Using dark NLP, you break people's behavior down into simple parts. Then you affect change by showing people how to behave differently. You use subtle influence to make people think about their actions and approach situations differently. Dark NLP essentially provides a tunnel directly into someone's mind. You can access their mind with simple techniques like sensory stimulus, gestures, and phrasing words in certain ways. Encouraging people to envision things and to think in new ways also enables you to change their thinking effectively.

And the best part about NLP? It is performed through simply nuances in speech or sensory stimulus. Therefore, it is undetectable. You can gain control over someone and he will never guess that you are the reason he is changing.

What You Need to Know

You need to know a few things about a person before you can make him change. You need to learn what he likes about himself, what he hates about himself, what he wants, what he fears, and what he has doubts about. These are essentially the elements of his identity, but they are also weak points. When you target them, you can change them? You can hurt someone through his doubts, fears, and dislikes, or disable him by removing all the things that he likes about himself and hopes for. You can also persuade or seduce him by playing on what he wants or scare him into action by provoking his fears. Do you understand now why these five things are so important to using dark NLP?

Take some time to get to know your victim before you employ dark NLP. Pay attention to what he does and says. The things that he talks about provide dead giveaways into what he feels and who he is. He will avoid what he fears and get nervous about what he doubts. He will get excited and brag about his hopes and his sources of pride. You will find plenty of clues into his identity if you just open your ears and listen carefully.

You can also coax someone into sharing themselves with you by talking about yourself. Share your own hopes, fears, doubts, and self likes and dislikes. When you open up, you establish a trusting bond. You also make him want to reciprocate. Listen to how he responds to you and pay attention to what he chooses to share with you.

You can find out someone's insecurities and pride by complimenting him. He will preen himself if you mention something that he likes about him. He will get rather shy and even hesitant to thank you when you compliment something that he is insecure about. This information is crucial to owning your victim.

Play on Hope and Fear

Play on someone's hopes and fears using your word choices. When you want to influence someone to act a certain way, you want to show him how it might be related to his hopes and how it will benefit him. On the other hand, remind him of his fears about an action that you want him to avoid.

You can also frame his perspective based on his hopes and fears. Use positive, upbeat language that relates to what he hopes for, or wants. For instance, if you want someone to date your sister, you want to paint a visual of your sister that includes all the things that this person hopes for in a partner. "She's kind, she loves to give love and compliments." Then you can flip this and hint that his worst fears will come true if he dates someone else that you don't want him to see. "She tends to emasculate men."

Play with someone's hopes and fears by offering them what they want and then confronting them with what they fear. This emotional roller coaster is confusing and also makes people insecure. They don't know which way is up when they are forced to experience so many different emotions. Fear and hope are two very powerful emotions, so using them simultaneously will have an impact on people emotionally.

Insult Someone Subtly

An obvious insult will make someone hate you. But subtle insults allow you to shatter someone's self-esteem while appearing innocent. Find out what someone hates about himself. Then mention that every now and then in a subtle way. Don't ever make a direct or obvious insult. Disguise your insults as compliments, even.

Chapter 7: Thoughts and Actions

Link between Thoughts, Decisions, Actions, and Results

There exists a strong link between your thoughts, decisions, actions, and reality. They form a never-ending cycle of reactions as your ideas influence your decision-making skills. Your choices shape the actions you take, and actions impact reality influencing thought patterns. So, it is safe to say that your thoughts also influence your reality. You will learn more about this interdependent relationship here.

There might have been times in your life where you look at a situation and wonder how you got there. At times, it could be something as simple as eating ice cream when you promised yourself you wouldn't. Other times, it could be a major decision with significant consequences, like impulsively quitting your job with nosafety net. To understand how your thoughts truly affectyour life, you need to understand their connection.

Thoughts

All the information around you is absorbed by the brain, which is then processed to form your thoughts. Your mind is essentially the gatekeeper of all the information present around you. It decides the relevance of this information and thereby decides which thoughts must get your mental focus. Thoughts can easily transform themselves into beliefs that influence our feelings. This influence can be negative as well as positive. Let us take the example of bingeing on ice cream. Perhaps the thought was simply, "I had a rough day, and I deserve something nice," or "I'm starving and this is my quickest option right now."

Feelings

Any emotional response to your thoughts or behaviors is known as a feeling. These act as indicators of your connection to a given situation. Feelings originate from past experiences as well as current perspectives. Things start getting a little tricky when you take a simple thought, "I am hungry," and add an emotional response to that thought. A lot of times we end up combining emotions from several other factors onto one specific thought, which really has nothing to do with that emotion. Thinking "I'm hungry," can have other connotations if linked to grief after receiving some bad news, stress from a hectic day, or anger from a fight.

Behaviors

The actions resulting from thoughts and feelings are known as behaviors. The way you behave is important because your thoughts are telling you that it is the best option at a given point. So, if you feel hungry, and feel stressed or sad, you might decide eating ice cream is the best way to deal with your emotions.

These three different aspects are interconnected, and one cannot exist without the other. So, when you start thinking about the impact your thoughts have, you will realize how much they affect your entire life. Thoughts not only trigger emotions but also guide your behavioral responses. Your perception of yourself and the world is altered by the way you feel. It, in turn, affects the way you respond to a given situation.

Your emotions and feelings guide your behavior, and your thoughts and beliefs guide your responses. You cannot act unless you have an idea on which you wish to initiate action and context as well. There's always a reason why we do the things that we do. Actions are never baseless, even if they seem completely random they are always caused by something even if you aren't aware of what. This something essentially relates to your feelings, emotions, thoughts, and beliefs. So, if you suddenly experience sadness, you might react in a specific way. If you feel angry or sad, your response will usually stem from your feelings at that moment. If you believe that someone should or should not do something, then your behavior might be triggered by your beliefs. For instance, if someone accidentally bumps into you, and you think they owe you an apology, and when they don't, your reaction if any will be triggered by your beliefs.

At times, you might be aware of any feelings or beliefs you have, and at times they are the result of underlying feelings you haven't processed yet. Feelings and beliefs don't appear out of thin air and have specific causes. They are generated from experience and starts from the moment you take your first breath until your last. Things will continue to happen, and we continue to come up with ideas about ourselves as well as the world around us. These experiences influence the way we feel about ourselves and the world.

For instance, a young child might be playing in the backyard, and after some time, decides to climb up a tree without success. Then, one day, he manages to scramble up the tree. He feels exuberant and triumphant in his success. He thinks it's the best time; he is having fun and feels safe. Then, suddenly, one of his parents comes out of the house and shouts at him for being in the tree. They tell him it's dangerous and he must never climb the tree again or will end up hurting himself. What is the child thinking at this moment? He is young, unsure, and doesn't fully understand the world around him so it could be any of the following:

- Having fun or feelings of fun are not safe.

- The world outside is dangerous.
- My parents don't want me to have fun.
- They are unhappy when I am having fun.
- I am not necessarily safe, even when I think I am.
- I will hurt myself if I have fun.
- It is dangerous to do things alone.
- It is not a good idea to try anything new.
- My parents don't think I can do anything.

As time passes, the child might forget the decisions he made or the belief that was formed because of it. Although he won't always recall that memory, it will be lodged in his subconscious in some way. Any other event or experience that reinforces this belief will slowly form his attitude towards life. So, there might be a time when the child is having fun with his friends and starts feeling uncomfortable about a good situation he is in. He starts to withdraw, and the previous belief he has formed about fun is preventing him from having it now. He might not even remember why he feels this way, but he knows he doesn't like it. As he grows up, he might think that he's not supposed to trust himself or the decisions he makes. And all this is because of a simple misunderstanding. This example, as mentioned earlier, is an instance of how beliefs are formed and the way they influence decision-making, actions, and results.

Once you understand the relationship between your thought process and actions, you give yourself a chance to choose your reactions. It, in turn, allows you to change because you know you have a choice. You can work on understanding your feelings, become more conscious about your decisions, and take action. There are three important things you must keep in mind while understanding this relationship.

The first thing you must do is validate your feelings. Regardless of what it is, never ignore the way things make you feel. If you wish to change something about yourself, the first step is to acknowledge and accept. If you feel sad or depressed, don't allow anyone to tell you otherwise. It is okay to feel sad or depressed. As soon as you accept your feelings, it becomes easier to work on changing them. When you understand what you feel and why you feel, you can take corrective action.

The second step is to guide your thinking. There's one thing you can always control, and that is the way you think. Your brain merely absorbs information, but it is a conscious decision to form thoughts. You can control your thoughts, and it must never be the other way around. If you allow your thoughts to control you, your life will become chaotic.

The third step is action. You cannot hold yourself accountable for the way you feel or the way you think. However, you can and will always be held responsible for the way you act. Your behavior, performance, actions, and the results are all dependent on you. If you get angry at someone and lash out physically, you will be held accountable for any altercation. Once you understand what it means to be accountable, it becomes easier to take corrective action. By merely changing the way you look at a problem, you can come up with a wide range of solutions.

Chapter 8: What is Emotional Manipulation?

You've likely experienced individuals who are emotionally manipulative and controlling.

They utilize these practices to get their direction or prevent you from saying or doing anything they don't care for.

Emotional manipulation can be unpretentious and misleading, leaving you befuddled and wobbly.

Or then again, it tends to be clear and requesting where fears, disgracing, and remorseful fits leave you shocked and immobilized.

In any case, emotional manipulation isn't worthy, and the more you enable it to proceed, the more force and certainty the manipulator gains in this uneven relationship.

Inevitably, any leftover of a sound association is pulverized, as the establishment of trust, closeness, regard, and security disintegrates under the sled of manipulation.

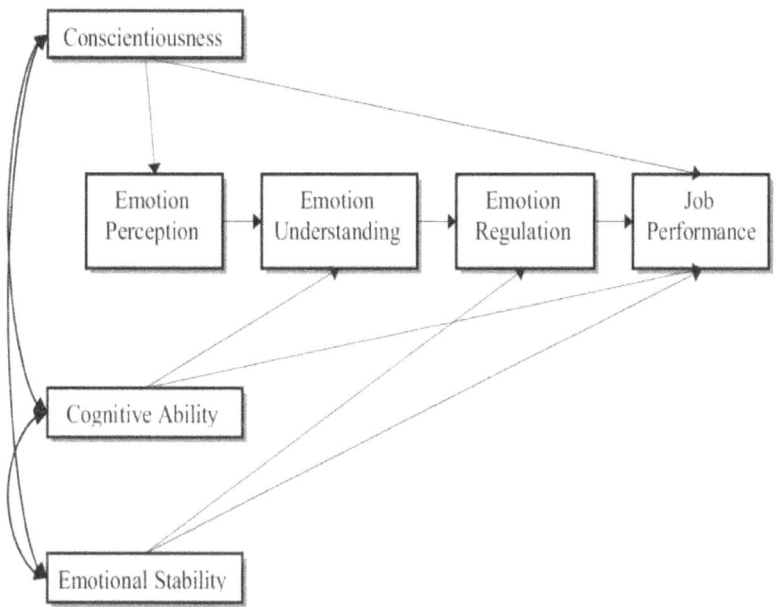

Specific Types of Emotional Manipulation

Within these major categories of emotional manipulation techniques, psychologists have also identified a wide range of more subtle variations that we all likely encounter daily.

These techniques include:

Lying

Dark Triad personalities, particularly psychopaths, are highly skilled at lying and cheating, so often we may not detect their intent until it is too late. Beware of those who have demonstrated a pattern of dishonesty.

Lying by Omission

Lying by omission is a little more subtle. The predator may not say anything untrue but may withhold information that is necessary for an effort to cause you to fail.

Denial

Often the damage from emotional manipulation is inflicted after the fact. When you confront someone with evidence of their dishonesty and abuse, their refusal to admit wrongdoing can cause even greater psychological harm.

Rationalization

The increase in popular news media has led to the growth of public relations and marketing firms who produce "spin" to deflect criticism in both political and corporate environments. A rationalization is a form of spin, in which a manipulator explains away his or her abuse.

Minimization

Like rationalization, a minimization is a form of denial in which the predator understates the seriousness of his or her offense.

Selective Attention and/or Inattention

Manipulators will pick and choose which parts of an argument or debate should be considered so that only their views are represented.

Diversion

Manipulators often resist giving straight answers to questions, particularly when they are confronted by their victims. Instead, they will divert the conversation to some other topic or change the subject altogether.

Evasion

More serious than a diversion, a manipulative person confronted with his or her own guilt will often completely evade responsibility by using long rambling responses filled with so-called "weasel words," like "most people would say," "according to my sources," or other phrases that falsely legitimize their excuses.

Covert Intimidation

Many manipulative people will make implied threats to discourage further inquiries or resolution.

Guilt-tripping

A true form of emotional manipulation, a manipulator will exploit the integrity and conscientiousness of the victim by accusing them of being too selfish, too irresponsible, or not caring enough.

Shaming

Although shaming can be used to bring about social change when large corporations or governments advance abusive or discriminatory policies, manipulators may attempt to intimidate their victims by using sharp criticism, sarcastic comments, or insults to make them feel bad.

Blaming the Victim

This tactic has become increasingly common. When a victim accuses a predator of abuse, the predator will attempt to turn it around by creating a scenario in which the victim alone is responsible for the harm that came to him.

Playing the Victim

Using the opposite tactic of blaming the victim, the predator will lure a conscientious person into a trap by pretending to have been grievously wounded and cultivating feelings of sympathy. The real plan, however, is to take advantage of the caring nature of the conscientious person by toying with their emotions.

Playing the Servant

This tactic is common in environments marked by a strict, well-established chain of command, like the military. Predators become skilled at manipulating this system by creating a persona of suffering and nobility, in which their bad actions are justified as a duty, obedience, and honor.

Seduction

This technique does not always have to involve sexual conquest or intimacy. Emotional predators may use flattery and charm to convince people to do their bidding, and they often look for people with low self-esteem.

Projection

This term is used in psychotherapy. Predators that use this technique will look for victims to use as scapegoats. When the manipulator does something wrong and is confronted, he or she will "project" his or her guilt onto the victim in an effort to make the victim look like the responsible party.

Feigning Innocence

This technique can be used as part of a strategy of denial. Under questioning, the manipulator will "play innocent" by pretending that any violation was unintentional, or that they were not the party who committed the violation.

Feigning Confusion

This technique can also be used as part of a strategy of denial. Under questioning, the manipulator will "play dumb" or pretend to be confused about the central point of the conflict or dispute. By creating confusion, the manipulator hopes to damage the confidence of his or her victim.

Peer Pressure

By using claims, whether true or not, that the victim's friends, associates, or "everyone else" is doing something, the manipulator will put pressure on his victim to change his or her behavior or attitude.

Signs That You're Being Manipulated

We are all potentially susceptible to emotional manipulation by people who show characteristic signs of dark psychology.

A very easy example can be Victimization: it can occur in our everyday relationships with co-workers, bosses and supervisors, family members, and significant others.

Emotional manipulation can also occur in professional relationships with people we may regard as normally trustworthy—such as sales representatives, government officials, and other representatives of institutions such as medical facilities, banks, businesses, schools, and law firms.

Emotional predators share one common trait: They look for people who are conscientious, dependable, loyal, honest, and reliable. People with these character traits are the easiest to manipulate because all the tricks in the manipulator's toolbox are designed specifically to take advantage of these emotional and psychological characteristics. More importantly, emotional predators lack empathy or morality. They do not regard their abuses as shocking or unacceptable; instead, they regard the overabundance of conscientious people as "job security" and a golden opportunity.

Emotional predators can be found in all walks of life. Throughout their lives, they have learned how to adapt, blend in, and even achieve high levels of professional and financial success in the "straight world."

Remember that having a valid and legitimate expectation that people will be honest in their dealings with you means that you are a conscientious person. Although you occupy the superior position, emotional predators are highly skilled at exploiting this expectation and avoiding detection and/or punishment.

As we have seen, emotionally manipulative people use a wide variety of techniques and methods to gain power in relationships. What's more, the people you are closest to and most familiar with—people whom you should be able to trust the most—are in the best position to use emotional manipulation to exploit and take advantage of your trust. In fact, establishing trust and familiarity is one of the most important aspects of a successful effort to exploit someone's emotional vulnerability, and then manipulate them either for personal gain or simply out of pure malice.

Of course, simply because this type of abuse has become common does not mean that you should automatically and necessarily regard all of your friends and trusted associates as predators and manipulators. Nor should you give in to the temptation to regard being conscientious, law-abiding, and honest as a problem. However, victims of emotional manipulation are often unaware that they are being exploited and abused, so it is important to learn how to recognize the signs of manipulation.

Specific Examples of Emotional Manipulation

- Insisting on meeting at certain locations: Manipulators may try to get the upper hand by insisting on a so-called "home-court advantage," thereby forcing you to function in a less familiar and less comfortable environment that diminishes your personal negotiating power. Examples:
    - If you have a dispute with a professional acquaintance or colleague, they may insist on always meeting in their office or at a café or restaurant that is more difficult for you to travel to.
- Premature intimacy or closeness: The manipulator will immediately shower you with affection and reveal all sorts of intimate secrets. Examples:
    - In a personal relationship, the manipulator may introduce themselves using phrases like, "No one has ever made me feel like this before. I know we were made for each other."
- Managing conversations by always requiring you to speak first: In professional relationships, this is commonly used as a sales and negotiation

technique to mine you for your information to make a more lucrative sale.

Examples:

- A salesperson may say something like, "Rather than bore you with details about our products or services, why don't you tell me about yourself and how you think we can help you?"

• Distorting or twisting facts: Whether in personal or professional relationships, manipulators will use conversational techniques to distort facts in an effort to make you doubt yourself and back down.

Example:

- A manipulator may use a phrase like, "I understand how you feel. I'd be angry, too. But the truth is, I never made that comment. I don't think your memory of that conversation is accurate. I know what you really meant to say was that..."

• Intellectual bullying: An emotional manipulator may use an unnecessarily large volume of statistics, jargon, or other types of factual evidence to impose a sense of expertise.

- Bureaucratic bullying: This technique is similar to intellectual bullying. Unfortunately, this technique may indicate that someone is abusing their position of authority by insisting on placing as many obstacles, red tape, or other impediments in the way of what should be a straightforward resolution.

    Example:
    - Such a person may make a statement such as, "I understand your concerns, but I would encourage you not to pursue this any further. You have a legitimate complaint, but the expenses and time required will probably cost more than you will get in return.

- Passive aggression: There are many examples of passive-aggressive behavior in conversation in both personal and professional relationships to force you to back down to the predatory efforts of a manipulator.

    Example:
    - A manipulator may try to make you feel bad for voicing your concerns by saying something along the lines of, "I understand that you are voicing an important objection, but have ever stopped to

consider what will happen to the rest of the team if you eventually get your way?"

- Insults and put-downs: Manipulators are good at following up rude or mean-spirited comments with sarcasm or some other attempt at humor to make it seem like they were joking.

Example:

  o "I know you really worked hard on that presentation. It's too bad you wasted your time, though. But, hey, no worries. I'm sure it will be great preparation when you interview for your position."

Chapter 9: Dark Criminals among Us

Before a person orchestrates something malicious, they may have thought about everything for a prolonged period, for instance, in the case of a mass shooting. The perpetrator's main motive may be unknown; however, it is evident upon investigation that such people have usually engaged in negative behaviors that are harmful to others close to them.

Some researchers, such as James Alan Fox and Monica J. DeLateur in their paper Mass Shootings in America: Moving beyond Newtown (2013), have looked into the matter, and the difficulty of identifying a potential mass shooter in advance, especially at a tender age. Nevertheless, it is evident that there are some thinking patterns and behaviors that usually manifest with time, and educators also encounter them since they spend a considerable amount of time with pupils. The parents are also familiar with each of these patterns. The main hope is that the children who exhibit each of these traits can outgrow them, eventually. Some children do; however, some do not outgrow these traits, and they can harm the people around them. When the patterns intensify, it is important to seek help, and we cannot wait for a seriously malicious action to occur.

When a person engages in crime at a tender age, it is a sign that there is some trouble ahead; not necessarily a mass shooting; however, the behaviors of such people may result in other people being financially, emotionally, and physically hurt.

People with Dark Triad traits may also engage in lying while also blaming other people for their misfortunes. The parents and teachers may not have the ability to control some of the choices that the children make; nevertheless, they may have noticed some warning signs.

Although Dark Triad traits manifest over time, children who simply exhibit some of these traits cannot be labeled as "criminals," since they have not doneanything wrong. Since the children are still young, theymay still be learning about the world, and they candevelop more understanding and empathy as they grow.They can turn out as good, well-rounded people, so it is important to support and work with them, without labeling children negatively.

Children are delicate beings, and they should be molded accordingly. When a child is born, people strive to look into whether the child may have learning problems, physical disabilities, and emotional problems. We should also strive to ensure that we have identified other problems that the children may be suffering from so that they cannot injure their peers or because any harm to themselves, since they do not have any sense of responsibility at a young age, this comes with learning and maturity.

The mental health system should be improved. There should be some strict background checks, and gun laws should also be revised. We should also focus more on identifying some of the "errors" present in the thinking process. We all possess enough knowledge about how we can help children who show potentially harmful traits. The children can be mentored accordingly, and they can hopefully develop more positive traits in the future. Always embark on such a mission with sensitivity and compassion.

Criminal Mind vs. Cybercriminal Mind

The study is related to criminal anthropology, and it delves deep into what drives someone into becoming a criminal. Additionally, the study also looks into a person's reactions after committing a crime.

Criminal psychologists are frequently called up to the stand in court so that they may serve as witnesses since they have an in-depth understanding of the criminal mind. There are different types of psychiatry, and they also deal with some aspects of criminal behavior. It is, however, somewhat difficult to define the criminal mind.

The Role of Psychology in the Legal System

Psychologists and psychiatrists are normally professionals who are licensed, and they are tasked with assessing the physical and mental state of a person. There are also profilers, and they are tasked with looking for patterns in a person's behavior as they try to identify the person who took part in a certain crime.

Some group efforts also focus more on attempting to answer different "common" psychological questions. If a sexual offender is about to commit a re-offending act after being put back into society, how can such an issue be handled? Other issues that arise include; is the sexual offender fit enough to take the stand in court? Was the offender sane when they were committing the offense?

A criminal psychologist may be required to undertake investigative tasks such as examining photographs that were taken at a crime scene. They can also be tasked with interviewing the victim and the suspect. At times, a criminal psychologist comes up with a hypothesis to assess what the offender might do after being released after they have completed their sentence.

The question about a person's competency to stand trial depends on the offender's state of mind as they engaged in the criminal act, and when they are about to take the stand in court. The criminal psychologist will have to assess the ability of the offender to understand the charges that have been placed against them and the possible outcomes that may arise after they are convicted. The offender should also have the ability to offer some assistance to their attorneys as they defend them in court.

The question of criminal responsibility is aimed at assessing the criminal's state of mind as they committed the crime. The main focus is on whether they understand the difference between what is right and wrong and anything that is against the law. The insanity defense is not commonly used, since it cannot be proved easily. If a person succeeds with the insanity defense, they will be sent to a secure hospital facility for a long period as compared to the period that they would have served in prison.

The Roles of a CriminalPsychologist

The roles of a legal psychologist are as follows:

Clinical

In such an instance, the psychologist is supposed to assess an individual so that they can issue a clinical judgment. The psychologist can make use of different assessment tools, psychometric tools, or they can take part in a normal interview with the offender. After that, they are supposed to make an informed decision depending on the outcome of the interview. The assessment comes in handy since it can help the police and other organizations to determine how the offender, in this case, will be processed. For instance, the clinical psychologist can find out whether the offender is sane so that they can stand a trial. They can also determine whether the offender has a mental illness, which relates to whether they are capable of understanding the court proceedings.

Experimental

In this instance, the psychologist is tasked with carrying out some research about the case. They can perform some experiments so that they can illustrate a certain point while also providing further information that will be presented as evidence in court. They may carry out eyewitness credibility and false memory assessments. For instance, they can try to assess whether an eyewitness can spot an object that is 100 meters away.

Advisory

A psychologist is supposed to advise the police about how they should proceed with the investigation. For instance, they can weigh into matters such as which is the best way to interview an eyewitness and the offender. They can also weigh into matters such as how an offender may act after committing a crime.

Actuarial

This is where the psychologist makes use of statistics so that they can inform a case. For instance, they can be tasked with providing the probability of an event taking place. The court may also consider the likelihood of a person engaging in certain acts such as defiling another person sexually after they have served their jail term or after they have been released if the evidence against them was not strong enough.

Profiling

Criminal profiling is also referred to as offender profiling. It is the process of linking the actions of an offender to the crime scene. The offender's characteristics will also ensure that the police can prioritize and narrow down all possibilities when considering all the possible suspects. Profiling is quite new concerning forensic psychology. The field of forensic psychology has grown in the past two decades. Initially, it was an art. Currently, it is a rigorous science. There are different sub-fields in forensic psychology, including investigative psychology. Criminal profiling currently entails carrying out some intensive research and also carrying out some rigorous methodological advances.

Criminals are usually classified based on factors such as sex, age, physical characteristics, geographic region, and education. When comparing some of the similar characteristics, you can easily understand a criminal's motivation when they decide to partake in criminal behavior.

Some national and international security organizations, including the FBI, usually refer to "criminal profiling" as "criminal investigative analysis." The analysts or profilers are normally trained. During the training process, they learn more about the behavioral aspects of different people and also learn more about the details of unsolved violent crime scenes, whereby there are some traces of psychopathy at the scene where the crime was committed.

The general appearance of the crime scene. It may be organized or disorganized.

The profiler can go ahead and interpret the behavior of the offender based on the crime scene. They can discuss everything further with their counterparts.

As a criminal psychologist, you may have to consider profiling from a racial perspective. Race plays a major role in the criminal justice system. In the past few years, the state and federal prisons have held more than 475,900 black inmates. The number of white inmates totaled 436,500. The difference is quite significant. Some of the black people are in prison because of negative stereotypes. Such stereotypes are ineffective, and some criminal psychologists can ascertain that the race of a person does not contribute to them being violent.

There are environmental, cultural, and traditional concepts that surround each race. Each of theseconcepts plays a key role in psychology. Some people may lack equal opportunities as a result of race or gender, for example, and that means that they have fewer chances to thrive.

Applied Criminal Psychology

For a criminal psychiatrist, the main question is, "Which offender will become a patient?" and "Which patient will become an offender?" Other questions that a psychiatrist should ask themselves are, "Which came first, the mental disorder or the crime?" Psychologists should take a look into the environmental factors and the genetics of a person while they carry out the profiling, to help determine whether the suspect committed the crime or not.

Some of the questions that criminal psychologists should ask themselves include:

- Is the mental disorder present at the moment? Did the person have a mental disorder when they were engaging in the criminal act?
- What is the level of responsibility of the person who committed the crime?
- Is treatment the best option when trying to reduce the risks of re-offending?
- Is there a possibility that the offender may engage in another crime, and what are the risk factors in this case?

Individual psychiatric evaluations normally come in handy since they help to measure an offender's personality traits through psychological testing. The results can also be presented in court.

Chapter 10: How the Mind Works When It Is Manipulated

When it comes to working with dark manipulation, there are going to be a lot of different methods and techniques that we can use to get what you want. Remember, we are talking about some forms of manipulation that are going to help us to get what we want but may end up harming the other person in the process. This means that they may not be seen as the best options to work with, and you may feel a bit uncomfortable with them if you have not worked in dark manipulation, or even with dark persuasion, in the past.

However, working with these techniques will help you to get the results that you want. They will ensure that the other person you are using as your target will be likely to do the actions or say the things that you would like them to, even though it may not be in their best interests to do so. With that said, let's take a look at some of the different dark manipulation tactics that you can use to get someone else to do what you want.

Using Isolation to Get What You Want

They like to spend some time talking with others, spending time out in public, having close friends, and family, and spending their time in more social situations. When we take this social aspect away from many individuals, it changes the way that they look at life.

Complete physical isolation can be the most powerful. This is when the subject is taken away from all contact with others, including email, social media, phone calls, and physical contact. This is something that has been seen in cults and with other groups. They will often take the person far away from others, and then the only human contact that the person can have is with the captors.

Now, this total physical isolation can be really hard to do, and it is usually only done in really intense situations. If you are just trying to use manipulation, you usually don't want to go through and completely isolate the target. But it is common for a manipulator will typically try to attempt their target mentally asmuch as possible.

There are several methods that the manipulator can use to get what they want with the help of manipulation. They could include some seminars that last a week in the country and isolate the person from what they would usually do. They could be a lot of criticisms of the person's family and close friends so that the target feels bad and stops seeing them. It could be jealousy that keeps the target at home and limits the amount of influence that anyone outside the manipulator has on the person.

Once the manipulator is able to control the information that goes to the target, they can share information, withhold information, and do anything that they would like in order to continue influencing the target as much as they would like. The target is going to become reliant on the manipulator, and this is how the manipulator can work and get what they want from the target. There are no outside influences to tell the target that something is wrong, or that they should watch out, and this ensnares the target even more.

Criticism

The next option to work with when it comes to manipulation is the idea of using criticism. This one is sometimes used with isolated or on its own and it works well because it makes the target feel like they are always doing something wrong, and that they are not able to meet the high standards of the manipulator. The criticism can always show up on a variety of topics and could include how they look, who they hang out with, the clothes they wear, their beliefs, and anything that the manipulator thinks will work for this.

When a manipulator decides to use this tactic, they are going to be really good at hiding it behind one of their compliments to the other person. Or they will say something nice and add this little jab at the end of it. This allows them to say all the mean things that they want, and then they can say that the target misheard or misunderstood them and that they hadn't really meant any harm by it. This puts the target in a bad spot because they know the manipulator is being mean to them, but they are the ones who look paranoid and bad in this situation.

The criticism that the manipulator is going to use is often going to be small. They don't want to start out using really big criticisms that are obvious because the target doesn't want to be criticized. If the manipulator starts out with something big, the target is going to fight back and walk away. But when it starts out small with some little comments along the way, it starts to plant a bit of self-doubt, something that the target is going to notice, but they often are not going to fight back against.

They are going to start out with something that may seem like a compliment or like that is going to sound like they are being helpful, but in reality, they are trying to be hurtful in the process. They may say something like, "I didn't know that you liked the color blue. I think you should go with something else." This one is going to have the hidden meaning inside of it that you don't look good in what you are wearing, and your clothes don't look that well.

Or maybe you bring in your favorite outfit to a meeting to make yourself feel better. You are excited and you feel really good about the way that you look and feel in the outfit. But then they are going to say something about how they liked you in some other outfit better. It isn't necessarily mean, but it is said in a manner and at a time that it ends up hurting your feelings in the process.

As time goes on, the type of criticism that is going to be used against the target is going to get worse. And the criticism is going to become quite a bit more obvious as well to add in a bit more self-doubt here. This is going to make it so that the target starts to rely on the manipulator a bit more. This is because the target is going to feel like they have so many flaws that are hard to ignore, and that the only person who can like them and maybe even love them, through these flaws will be the manipulator. The fact that the manipulator is still around is a good sign that they care, and this causes the target to be more willing to do what the manipulator asks.

The manipulator is going to find that they are able to use this criticism more of us against them kind of idea if it works better as well. They could even choose to move their criticism to be against the outside world so that they can claim they are more superior.

When this happens, the manipulator is going to claim to their target that they are super lucky that the manipulator is even associating with them. The manipulator will ensure that they are important so that the target is more likely to stick around and do what they want. This alone is meant to be enough if it is done in the right manner so that the target feels lucky just because the manipulator is going to spend time with them.

Alienating the Target to Get What They Want

No one wants to be alienated. They want to feel like they are a part of the group. They want to feel accepted, as they belong, and more. This is never more apparent than when we see a newcomer. When someone is new to town, or to school, to work, or somewhere else, you will notice that they are trying to figure out how to join the group and get them to accept them. They are worried that they are going to be alienated and to avoid this, they will do everything in their powers to get others to like them and go along with them, and this is where the manipulator can come in and get what they want.

Newcomers who start to join a new manipulative group are usually going to receive a very warm welcome.

There are several reasons for this one. First, this gets the target to feel welcome and more indebted to the group and the manipulator. They are thankful that they have these deep connections, and it is usually easier to get a friend to go along with something that a stranger, so it works to the benefit of the manipulator as well. Add in that the target is scared to be alienated, then they are going to do what they can to keep the relationships going strong.

If any doubts end up arising, these relationships are going to become a powerful tool to ensure they stay with the group. Even if they aren't completely convinced, the target will start to remember their outside world, the world that they had before joining this group, and it is going to seem cold and lonely. They will instead choose to stay with the group, even if there is some manipulation going on.

Simply because we do not want to be taken away from the crowd and we don't want others to have anything to do with us, we are going to do what the manipulator wants us to. The fact that humans are very social creatures and like to be included in some kind of group all the time, it is likely that we are going to give in to these urges to do what the manipulator wants, even if we don't feel like it is the best thing for us.

Using Social Proof as a Form of Peer Pressure

We like it when we are able to be a part of the group. Sometimes we center this on wanting to fit in, and we will follow the rules and do what we can to make sure that we are liked and part of the group. And even when we are more introverted and don't want to be in the group all the time, we still want to find a group of people we can be around and fit in. The thing is that the manipulator is able to come in here and use the idea of wanting to fit in to help them work against you and get you to do things that you don't want to.

Chapter 11: The Role of Defense

To avoid falling victim to manipulators, you have to build your defenses so that you are prepared for any manipulative strategies that they may try to use on you. The best way to build your defenses is by taking steps to improve your self-esteem and your willpower. However, as a point of caution, you should be very careful about how you build your defenses because you don't want to create restrictions that will keep you from living a fulfilled life.

For example, as you try to guard against manipulation, you can't act out of fear. You can't hide from the world just to avoid scenarios where someone might want to take advantage of you. Remember that the world is full of people with dark personality traits who may harbor malicious intentions, so acting out of fear won't protect you from anyone. In fact, it will just make you more of a target. As you build your defenses, make sure that start on the premise that you are willing to confront manipulators head-on, and you will never run away or recoil. If you act out of fear, you lose by default.

The Steps to Raise Self-Esteem

To help you build your defenses, we will discuss the eight steps that you have to take to raise your self-esteem and to increase your willpower by extension.

Acceptance

Acceptance is about assenting to the reality of a given situation. It's about recognizing that a certain condition or process is what it is, even if it's characterized by high levels of discomfort and negativity. It's about consciously submitting to the fact that something cannot be changed, and that its reality is not subject to interpretation. It's about making peace with the situation that you are in.

Acceptance is the opposite of denial. Even the most rational among us tend to be in denial about lots of things in their lives, which are settled facts in the real sense. Denial can be a coping mechanism, one that can keep us from being overwhelmed by the reality of a given situation. However, denial does us more harm than good, because unless we can accept something, we can't change it, and we will be stuck looking for alternative interpretations and explanations for our prevailing circumstances.

Without acceptance, the door remains wide open for malicious people to exploit us. Take the example of a patient who is told that he/she is terminally ill. After seeking the opinions of several medical professionals and getting the same diagnosis, the patient is still left with the choice of either accepting or denying the situation. The one who accepts it will make peace and try to make the best out of what little time he has. The one who stays in denial will become susceptible to tricksters, who may offer "alternative cures," and he may end up losing all his savings paying such people so that in the end, he leaves his family with nothing. That is an extreme example, but it perfectly illustrates why acceptance is important in avoiding manipulation, even if the reality may seem too painful to accept.

The most crucial form of acceptance is self-acceptance. It refers to the state of being satisfied with yourself, the way you currently are. Most people have trouble accepting themselves as they are. We are all in a constant strive for self-improvement. We want to be more successful, to be wealthier, to be more attractive, or to be perceived more positively by others. Even the most accomplished among us have issues with self-acceptance.

In many ways, the desire to be a better version of yourself can be seen as a positive thing; it can help you study harder in school, work harder to earn a promotion at work or exercise more to get in shape. However, the problem is there is always room for improvement, so no matter how high you ascend, the dissatisfaction will always be there, and it will make you vulnerable to manipulation by people who want to take advantage of your desires.

To defend against manipulation, you have to accept your reality, and you have to accept yourself. People tend to think that if they accept themselves, they won't try to improve—that couldn't be further from the truth. Accepting yourself means owning up to your flaws, and that gives you control over your life. With self-acceptance, attempts at self-improvement would come from within, so when you decide to change, you will be doing it for yourself and not for anyone else.

Increase Awareness

Increasing your awareness means having a higher level of alertness when it comes to understanding what's going on in your environment. It means paying close attention to your surroundings, and to the way people behave around you. The higher your level of awareness, the better you will be when it comes to adapting to your surroundings and understanding the motivations of the people you interact with.

When you become more aware, you will be able to catch on quickly when people try to manipulate you. Many of us tend to be preoccupied with our own thoughts that we hardly ever notice the cues of the people we interact with. We tend to live life on autopilot, so when other people try to seize control over our lives, we only notice it when it's too late. If you increase your awareness, you will be equipped with the skills necessary to identify all the red flags, and you will be able to stop most manipulators on their tracks before they can do any real harm.

The first step towards increasing your awareness is to learn about the tendencies of manipulative people. You now know enough to be able to spot people with ill motives, but you should understand that the worst kinds of manipulators are very good at concealing their motives, so you have to keep working on increasing your awareness.

To be truly aware of manipulative people, you have to approach all interactions with some levels of skepticism. We are not telling you to turn into a paranoid person who doesn't let anyone in; we are just saying that you should take a deeper look at each person you interact with. Try to study their body language and their words, and try to see if they are trying to hide something.

Apart from increasing your awareness, you have to increase your self-awareness as well. Many people confuse those two things, but they are entirely different concepts. Self-awareness is about understanding yourself. It's about having a clear concept of your own personality. You have to examine yourself and figure out what your strengths and weaknesses are, what your values and motivations are, and what kind of thoughts and emotions you are likely to have in specific situations. Self-awareness helps you understand both who you are and how other people perceive you.

Self-awareness works as a defense against manipulation because when you know who you truly are, it becomes more difficult for someone to alter your thoughts and perceptions. If you have strong and well-articulated values, it becomes harder for a manipulator to get you to abandon those values. People who like self-awarenessare more likely to be gaslighted or to be subjected to other forms of mind control.

If you end up in a relationship with a manipulative person, self-awareness can help you keep your identity. Manipulators will try to tell you what to think and how to behave, but if you are self-aware, you will experience cognitive dissonance, and your brain will push back against any attempts at manipulation.

Detach with Love

Detaching with love is a defense against manipulation that is most commonly used by people who have loved ones who suffer from substance abuse problems. Even though it was conceptualized to help people deal with addicts, it can also work when you are dealing with manipulators.

Detaching with love is about showing love and compassion for others without taking responsibility for their actions. For example, if you have a family member who is a drug addict, the way it works is that you try to support them and encourage them to get clean, but you let them make their own decisions, and you let them suffer the consequences of their actions. If the addict doesn't come home, you don't waste your time looking for them in the seedy parts of the city, you stay at home, and you do the things that benefit you and make you happy.

The point of detaching with love is to stop trying to control other people's lives, even if you are doing it for their own good. The idea is that you accept that people are different from you and that they have their own free will.

Detaching from love can defend you from manipulation in many ways. Some manipulators want to exploit you by making you responsible for them. They want you to give them all your attention; that is how they control you.

When you detach with love, you will learn to stop fixing everyone's problems. So, when the manipulator tries to play the victim to gain your sympathy, you will keep doing whatever is in your best interest, and you will tell him or her to take responsibility for his or her own actions.

Some manipulators may take up self-destructive habits because they want to dominate you by making you clean up after them. When they do this, you can detach with love by letting them follow the paths they have taken, no matter where they lead them. If they are causing you harm, you can get away from them, but leave your door open. If they find the right path in the future and regain control over their own lives, you can let them in again. You have to make it very clear, through your words and actions that you will let them direct their own lives, and you won't take any responsibility for them.

Detaching with love is about accepting others for who they are and respecting them enough to let them be in charge of changing their own lives. When you feel responsible for someone, and he makes a choice that harms you both, oftentimes, you will react with fear, anger, or anxiety. To detach with love, you have to learn to let go of those negative emotions.

Manipulators count on the fact that you will react in a predictable way to their machinations, but when you detach with love, you learn to calm yourself down and think about your role in the other person's life before you take any sort of action. This will keep you from falling into the traps that manipulators will set for you.

Detaching with love builds your self-esteem because it allows you to put your own needs ahead of those of the people that try to manipulate you.

Chapter 12: Toxic People

You can identify toxic persons by their behavior. Some relationships are also found to be toxic. Toxic people are suffering deep within, and they cannot take care of their problems. The person cannot meet their needs and feelings. They suffer from these ungratified needs and desires. To ease the suffering, they are experiencing the persons, behave in outrageous ways and their lives are one huge dramatic comedy. They cover up their wounded nature by portraying themselves as martyrs, perfectionists, bullies, and victims of circumstances. They also try these behaviors as they seek to satisfy their needs and heal from the wounds they sustained earlier in their lives.

These persons are dramatic, and they thrive in environments filled its drama. The person enjoys the attention they get from acting out. As a result, the person will magnify the insignificant issues and overreact causing others to turn heads. With little to show off for in terms of personal achievements, the person feels irrelevant and invisible. Since the person wants to gain some recognition, they will seek drama in every situation to refocus others' attention. They are also needy, demanding attention all the time from everyone in their lives.

Toxic persons are also manipulative as they use other people to have their needs met. When you grow close to a toxic person, they will find ways to make you do things for them. They will fake illnesses to seek sympathy, which they use to benefit themselves. The person will act as a victim of his or her past. They will use their self-perceived wounds as an excuse for their outrageous behaviors and habits. The person is already aware of their weaknesses, and they do not want to lose your friendship along with its benefits, they will devise ways of manipulating you to stick close. They also enjoy controlling others to have them worshipping them and doing different tasks for them. Toxic people will enslave you by their demands and manipulative techniques, and if you are not aware of what is happening, you will lose yourself while trying to save them.

Toxic persons find faults in everything and everyone. They pass harsh judgment and criticism on themselves and others. The person cannot focus on positive things.

They are also unable to expect positive outcomes. Even with such negative expectations, the person will not like the negative outcomes. They blame themselves and are too aware of their weaknesses. They will want to concentrate on their shortcomings and hardly see any significance in their strengths. The person fails to understand that no one is perfect, as we are all designed with weak points and strong points. When the person fails to recognize the strengths they hold, they are less likely to make an effort to discover their talents and unique abilities that are everyone's building blocks for success.

Toxic persons are also envious of others' achievements as they believe others are jealous of them too. They live in desperation, as they are always comparing themselves with others. The person lives in a moan-full mood as they compare other good fortunes with their misfortunes. It becomes difficult for such a person to see any beauty in their lives. The persons believe others are more advantaged, and they resent people who are doing better than them.

Toxic persons are more likely to hurt themselves because they do not find any value in their lives. The person has limited motivation, no goals, or plans for their future. These people also cause harm to others. They are at a higher risk of involving themselves in drugs. Such persons will hardly seek help as they don't view themselves as deserving of anyone's attention.

Toxic people are persistent in their demands, and however much you turn them down, they will persist. The person has no regard for the other person's values and personal principles. They are out to make others act out of their norm.

When having an interaction with a toxic person, your reaction to their words and behavior can lead to your acquiring toxicity. You need to watch your reactions and avoid losing your values to satisfy the person's demands. In such interactions don't lash out at theother person out of frustration, as it will result in dramain which you do not want to participate. You might alsowalk out on the other person once they start throwing negative remarks your way, which is an inferior way of facing challenges.

When in a relationship or friends with a toxic person, your life is chaotic in many ways:

You are in are always fixing the person's endless problems. Toxic people are attention seekers, and they will want to have others involved in sorting out their issues that seem to occur more often than normal. Some of the problems are of their creation as they attempt to have people around caring for them.

You are not comfortable with your own life and your progress in your goals. Friendship with toxic persons can ruin your life by diverting you from your personal purposes. The person demands all the attention they can get from you. If you are not cautious, you will set aside your goals and live to satisfy the person's demands. The negativity of the person can overcrowd your positivity, draining you out of your positive energy.

You feel exhausted following interaction with them. Toxic persons are tedious to deal with. Their constant demands will drain you physically and emotionally. You will listen to the person to complain about the least significant issues. Their views of others and life, in general, will haunt your intelligence.

Having them around fills you with anxiety. When you have a toxic person in your life; either family or close friend and you do not want to isolate from them, you have no choice but to tolerate them. You will experience anxiety when you are about to meet them because you would rather not. As you anticipate their behavior and attitude, you can't wait to get it over with.

You feel drained from their constant drama. Toxic people enjoy causing a scene as it draws others' attention. Whenever you are with the person; you are sure at some point they will over-react, causing others to focus their attention on you. If you are a nontoxic person, the experience will not be as thrilling. You will avoid interacting with the person, especially in a public setting because you do not want to be caught up in their drama.

When you are with the person, you feel as if you are getting out of touch with your being. You are either pushed around too much or reacting by controlling the toxic person. Toxic people have the habit of being too pushy. When you are driven to the edge by their persistence and demands you will result in acting too controlling to prevent them from pushing and dragging you around at their free will.

You also feel overly self-conscious and cautious. When in the company of toxic people, you can't predict what to expect from them. Their behaviors are rather shameful to an average person. You always feel like you are walking on glass.

How Negative and Toxic People Affect Your Life

Toxic and negative people are bound to infect you with their negative outlook on life. Their thoughts highly influence the behaviors of a person.

Interactions with others can also result in toxic relationships which are defined by the following;

Managing Negative Thoughts

Personal views and beliefs held by a person are a result of life-time experiences. Our beliefs are influenced by the environment we grew up in and other societal factors. Changing personal beliefs is a challenge because they make up our being. A person can't see any faults in their belief systems. Thought patterns are not easily notable either.

A person can manage negative thoughts in the following ways:

Start by consciously acknowledging the negative thoughts as they occur in your mind. When facing challenges, you will note your thought patterns shifting from solution seeking to self-defeating thoughts.

Once you have identified these negative thoughts, you can easily challenge them. Challenging our ideas involves trying to find enough evidence to support our conclusions. In challenging negative thoughts, we learn to introduce rational questioning in them. We look at the evidence in terms of the credibility of the source of this evidence; is the evidence we are basing our conclusion on credible? How trustworthy is the source of the information on which we are basing our conclusions? Are there facts supporting the evidence? Are these facts accurate? The answers to these questions will help us in passing judgment on the validity of our thoughts. Thoughts that are not substantiated enough should be discarded.

The following step involves replacing the negative thoughts with more positive ones. By embracing the positive thoughts and letting go of the negative, the person is effectively able to train the brain to focus on positivity. The challenging of negative thoughts might seem difficult to follow through, but over time it becomes natural for the person. People who have adopted the otherwise termed as Socrates questioning are always questioning the validity of their conclusions on decisions, and it helps them ineffective critical decision making.

Chapter 13: How to Fake Your Body Language

Regardless of being in the workplace or out with our partners, the non-verbal communication of the people around us says a lot. Peruse the full article to gain proficiency with every one of the eight regular non-verbal communication signals.

Concentrate on the Eyes - Eye Conduct Can Be Telling

Powerlessness to look can demonstrate fatigue, lack of engagement, or even misdirection—particularly when somebody turns away and to the side. If an individual looks down, then again, it regularly shows anxiety or accommodation. Students expand when subjective exertion increments, so if somebody is centered on a person or thing they like, their understudies will consequently widen.

Understudy enlargement can be hard to recognize; however, under the correct conditions, you ought to have the option to spot it. Now and again, the expanded flickering rate demonstrates lying—particularly when joined by contacting the face (especially the mouth and eyes). Looking at something can recommend a longing for that thing. For instance, if somebody looks at the entryway, this may demonstrate a craving to leave.

Looking at an individual can show a longing to converse with the person in question. Regarding eye conduct, it is likewise proposed that looking upwards and to one side during discussion shows an untruth has been told while looking upwards and to one side demonstrates the individual is coming clean. The purpose behind this is individuals turn upward and to one side when utilizing their creative mind to come up with a story, and gaze upward and to one side when they are reviewing a genuine memory.

Look at the Face - Body Language Touching Mouth or Smiling

Give specific consideration to the mouth when attempting to disentangle non-verbal conduct.

An authentic grin recommends that the individual is glad and getting a charge out of the organization of the individuals around the person in question.

You may likewise see a slight scowl that endures not exactly a second before somebody grins. Tight, pressed together lips likewise show disappointment, while a casual mouth demonstrates a casual demeanor and positive temperament. Covering the mouth or contacting the lips with the hands or fingers when talking might be a pointer of lying.

Focus on Vicinity

The vicinity is the separation between you and the other individual. Focus on how close somebody stands or sits alongside you to decide whether they see you positively. Standing or sitting in closeness to somebody is maybe probably the best marker of affinity. You can enlighten a great deal regarding the sort of relationship two individuals have simply by watching the closeness between them.

Check Whether the Other Individual Is Reflecting You

Reflecting includes mirroring the other individual's non-verbal communication. When interfacing with somebody, verify whether the individual mirrors your conduct. For instance, if you are sitting at a table with somebody and lay an elbow on the table, hold up 10 seconds to check whether the other individual does likewise. Another basic reflecting motion includes tasting a beverage simultaneously. If somebody copies your non-verbal communication, this is a generally excellent sign that the person is attempting to build up compatibility with you. Take a stab at changing your body stance and check whether the other individual changes theirs correspondingly. Watch the head development

The speed at which an individual gestures their head when you are talking demonstrates their understanding—or absence of. Slow gesturing demonstrates that the individual is keen on what you are stating and needs you to keep talking. Quick gesturing demonstrates the individual has heard enough and needs you to complete the process of talking or give that person ago to talk. Tilting the head sideways during the discussion can be an indication of enthusiasm for what the other individual is stating. Tilting the head in reverse can be an indication of doubt or vulnerability. Individuals likewise point with the head or face at individuals they are keen on or share a partiality with. In gatherings and gatherings, you can tell who the individuals with power depend on how regularly individuals take a gander at them. Then again, the less-critical individuals are taken a gander at less frequently.

Take a Quick Check at the Other Individual's Feet

A piece of the body where individuals regularly "release" significant non-verbal signals is the feet. The reason individuals unexpectedly convey non-verbal messages through their feet is that they are generally so centered around controlling their outward appearances and chest area, situating that significant pieces of information are uncovered using the feet. When standing or sitting, an individual will, for the most part, point their feet toward the path they need to go. So and when you see that somebody's feet are pointed toward you, this can be a decent sign that they have a positive assessment of you.

This applies to one-on-one collaboration and gathering association. You can enlighten a ton regarding bunch elements just by contemplating the non-verbal communication of individuals included, especially what direction their feet are pointing. What's more, and when somebody has all the earmarks of being occupied with discussion with you, yet their feet are pointing toward another person, it's presumable the person would prefer to converse with that individual (in any case if the chest area signals recommend something else).

Watch for Hand Signals

Like the feet, the hands release significant non-verbal signals when looking at non-verbal communication. This is a significant hint when perusing non-verbal communication, so give close consideration to this. Watch non-verbal communication turns in pockets when standing. Search for specific hand signals, for example, the other individual placing their hands in their pockets or hand on head. This can show anything from apprehension to inside and out duplicity.

Oblivious pointing demonstrated by hand motions can likewise say a lot.

When making hand signals, an individual will point in the general heading of the individual they share a partiality with (this non-verbal prompt is particularly essential to look for during gatherings and when connecting in gatherings). Supporting the head with the hand by laying an elbow on the table can demonstrate that the individual is tuning in and is keeping the head still to center. Supporting the head with the two elbows on the table, then again, can show weariness.

At the point when an individual holds an article between the person in question and the individual they are associated with, this fills in as an obstruction that is intended to shut out the other individual. For instance, if two individuals are talking, and one individual holds a stack of paper before that person, this is viewed as a blocking demonstration in non-verbal correspondence.

Look at the Situation of the Arms

Think about an individual's arms as the entryway to the body and oneself. If an individual folds their arms while interfacing with you, it is generally observed as a protective, blocking motion. Crossed arms can likewise show nervousness, powerlessness, or a shut personality. Whenever crossed arms are joined by a veritable grin and by and large loosened up stance, at that point, it can demonstrate a sure, loosened up frame of mind. When somebody puts their hands on their hips, it is normally used to apply predominance and is utilized by menmore regularly than ladies.

Is non-verbal communication a "learnable aptitude," and can it in this manner be faked? The appropriate response is yes and no. Most by far of the more common non-verbal communication can be scholarly. For instance, keeping your hands out of your pockets or utilizing the hands expressively to stay legitimate and open, or repelling the hands from the face to appear to be increasingly certain as effectively learned through cognizant idea and redundancy. In any case, another zone of study uncovers that there is an entirely different arrangement of signs that are significantly harder to control, if certainly feasible.

A Wrinkled Brow Can Occur in a Brief Instant and Uncover Negative Feelings

These are called micro-expressions or micro-signals. These signs can be utilized to disentangle liars from truth-tellers. Micro-expressions show up as wrinkles, grins, glares, grins, and wrinkles and can offer a precise, however short-lived, window into feelings. These micro-expressions are constrained by muscles, for example, the frontalis, corrugator, and risorius, and they are incited by hidden feelings that are difficult to control deliberately. One of these feelings is the phony grin to demonstrate submission instead of certifiable euphoria or joy. The phony grin is self-evident because the lips are pulled over the mouth, yet the muscles controlling the eyes have no influence.

With particular PC programming, specialists have had the option to identify these signs. PCs were utilized because the sign moves quickly over the face in divisions of seconds, making it difficult for people to lift the sign deliberately.

Hindering video on rapid camcorders and playing it back over and over to spectators can likewise be utilized to distinguish the articulations. So some portion of the story is that micro-expressions are hard to recognize and control, yet the remainder of the story discloses to us that if they exist (and they do), that we should at some level have advanced the capacity to peruse and distinguish them. Along these lines, we should be mindful about accepting that since they happen so quickly, that they can't be gotten and on the other hand that we can without much of a stretch phony our way through the non-verbal channel. It could be that the subliminal instinct is working diligently, giving us that intuition feeling that can't confide in somebody despite not exactly having the option to put it to words. The reason, it appears, is a blend of micro-expressions and our instinct.

A few scientists will disclose to us that the face is the most straightforward piece of our bodies to control, yet this isn't valid and is a sorry excuse for the full story. If our countenances were so effectively controlled, why have Botox medicines to stop up our appearances with low-level poisons to eradicate wrinkles? Why not simply quit utilizing the muscles out and out and, in this way, abstain from experiencing facial wrinkles during the maturing procedure? The straightforward answer is that it's not the basic.

While our countenances are in certainty under an enormous part under our influence, we can't generally be centered around it, in case we do not have the option to concentrate on whatever else. Not the least of which is controlling our discourse. Would you be able to envision what it resembles to build sentences freestyle while attempting to stay expressive and yet abstain from contracting "unseemly" facial muscles (whatever they may be)? When we talk or see, or do, our faces normally react to what is happening around us since they are firmly attached to our psyche and our feelings. It is circumstances and logical results relationship, or even a weapons contest, and it correctly because the face gives such an immense measure of data that we are so fixed on understanding it.

Different approaches to detect phony concerns incongruent non-verbal communication. That is, a language that is conflicting with either the words being communicated in and the non-verbal language that goes with it.

Chapter 14: Undetected Mind Control

Your mind is your sanctuary. No matter what else can be lost to others, the mind is yours and yours alone. Or so we think. People like to believe that they are the ones in control of their own actions and thoughts. Many times our minds can be susceptible to the influence of others, and this allows others to control our minds if we're not careful.

Think about a time when you watched a horror movie. Your mind and your emotions are already being led and influenced in the movie. All the decisions of the director, from the camera shot, the lighting, and the music can determine how you are going to feel and react. Even though you are in full awareness that you are just watching a movie, the brain is going to respond to the prompts when they are given. If our brain can be so influenced by something that we are aware of, how strong would the influence of a dark manipulator be?

Undetected mind control is often the most deadly type of mind control there is. If someone is already aware that their mind is being influenced, then they have the option to object, either physically, verbally, or mentally. For example, they can choose to avoid any contact with the person who controls them. A lot of people are going to run at the first sign they see a dangerous person trying to get inside the brain and take over. But if the mind controller is able to get into the brain of their victim without the victim detecting them, then the victim has no chance to put up their defenses before it's too late.

There are going to be two tactics that the manipulator can use to take over the mind of their victim without detection. This includes the use of media and interpersonal interactions. Traditionally, the media mind control was only possible for the larger company. Most individual mind controllers were left to deal with just the interpersonal interactions. But with the changes in technology now, this is no longer the case.

Smartphones and laptops have allowed even individual manipulators to have media mind control. This can make it a very powerful tool that the manipulator can use. While the undetected mind controller is going to be able to use all these methods, they are often going to be more deliberate and only take their actions after some careful consideration. They are sometimes seen as a big more coward compared to some other controllers, such as psychological manipulators, but they will take deliberate actions in order to find the right victim to do the attack on.

Undetected Mind Control Tactics

Now that we know a little bit more about undetected mind control, it is time to learn about some of the methods that are used by manipulators to control the mind of a victim in an undetected way. We are going to explore both the media and the interpersonal techniques that are in the toolkit of the manipulator. Let's take a look at some of the different undetected mind control tactics.

Finding Those Who Are in Need

The first principle that comes with undetected mind control is to find a victim who has a goal. It has been proven that a person who has a pressing desire or needs is someone who will be more susceptible to this type of mind control compared to someone that feels satisfied and at ease. This could range from a small physical goal, such as someone thirsty and looking for a drink. Or it can be a more psychological goal, such as someone who is craving affection and love.

A good example of this is the experiment that was conducted to look at a subliminal influence or undetected mind control. In this study, there were two sets of people who were shown a film, but this film had a hidden image of iced tea. One set of people in the study were thirsty, and the second group wasn't.

After the movie, when the participants were given the chance to purchase a specific drink from a selection, the ones who were thirsty would purchase the iced tea in greater numbers compared to those who weren't thirsty. This shows that, when the brain is desperate for something, they are gladly taking suggestions on what they should choose.

So, how would you be able to use this principle with an individual on more of an interpersonal level? If the mind controller is able to find a victim who is already craving something in their life, then the manipulator will find that it is easier to control that victim. One example is a victim who just got out of a long-term relationship. They may crave the company again and the mind controller would be able to influence their target into thinking that they are the savior for the victim. In reality, they are going to cause harm and even ruin for the victim, but the victim will crave attention so much that they will fall for the mind control that is put on them.

There are a lot of needs that a manipulator is going to seek to exploit their victim, including their need for company, their need to belong, and even monetary stability. These vulnerabilities are going to be exploited by someone who is more experienced for many purposes. They may want to financially or sexually exploit the victim. They may want to gain the victim's allegiance to form a cult or other extreme movement. Some manipulators just go through this process to toy with their chosen victim for their own pleasure.

Media Control with Images

Just like our five senses can be guides in our lives, they can also be our enemies. Our sense of sight is very powerful. This is why we can even dream visually, even when all the other senses are missing, and we can use our sight to see images of past memories. This can make imagery as well as visual manipulation, a really powerful technique to use with media mind control.

Because of the changes in technology, impactful imagery techniques are in the hands of manipulators allover the place, and they can even take these techniques and tailor them to their specific victims. So, if their victim seems to have a fear or an aversion to something, the manipulator is able to use the feared images to helpaccess and then warp the emotions of a person without the victim even realizing what's going on.

Let's look at how this type of mind control can work. We are in an age where there are lots of smartphones, videos, and more. Everything is shot in high definition clips and can be sent at fast speeds to someone else. This means that a high-tech manipulator can allude to the feared image. For example, if a manipulative boyfriend knows that his girlfriend has a big fear of insects, they could "accidentally" put a book with a picture of an insect on its cover in the background somewhere during that video chat. While the girlfriend may not consciously register that the book is there, on an emotional and subtle level, she is going to feel the impact.

Restricting Choice

Restricting choice is another form of undetected mind control. It can be a subtle form of this because it is going to provide the manipulator with a range of built-in "get out clauses" if the victim ever starts to get suspicious. The key to this type of mind control is to take away any real choices that the victim has in a specific circumstance, while still providing the illusion that the victim is the one who has the control.

Let's say that there is a woman who is being asked to go out on a date. A regular guy is going to spend some time to ask the question and then stammer out an open-ended question. They may say something like "Would you like to go out with me?" This question allows the woman to say yes or no based on their personal preferences. This is the way that people who aren't using manipulation will behave.

But someone who is trying to use mind control will approach all of this differently. They will confidently and smoothly work to charm the victim. They will get that person to laugh a bit and lower their guard. Then, with a lot of confidence and assurance, the manipulator will ask something like "So, am I taking you out on Thursday or Saturday?" This limits the choices that the victim can go with. The answer of no really isn't an option here, so the victim will pick one of the dates they are given. The victim can't really say that they weren't in control, but the manipulator had complete control the whole time.

Now, if the manipulator is caught, or the victim realizes that they are limited on the choices they are allowed to make, the manipulator can backtrack and still look innocent. They could say something to their victim like, "I can't believe you're analyzing my words so much. That really hurts me and makes me not want to open upto you." This can make the victim feel like they were being meant, and they will probably give in.

Media Mind Control with Sound

Sound is another method that the manipulator can use in order to do mind control. But personal experience and experiments can confirm this. Have you ever had a song that seems to get stuck in your head? How easy did you find it to get that song out of your head? The sound may have had a big influence on you, even though you knew it was there.

The power of audio manipulation is even greater when it is undetected. Experiments have shown that if customers are exposed to music that comes from a specific region, then they are more likely to order wine from that country. When they were questioned about it later, they had no idea that the sound around them was what influenced them for their decision making.

While there are examples of the media mind control with sound in the media and with the government, even individual manipulators are able to use this kind of mind control as well. One of the creepiest forms of this mind control is to influence the victim when they are asleep subliminally. A skilled mind controller can get their victim when that victim is at the most vulnerable, such as when they are sleeping, and then can implant the dark and devious commands in the ear of their victim. This allows the commands to sink into the lowest layers of the brain of that victim.

Another form of this auditory mind control is to mask the words with other words or noises that sound similar.

Sounds that are outside the range of human perceptions can be this type of mind control.

Chapter 15: Effects of Narcissism in Relationships

You know you shouldn't fall in love with a narcissist, but somehow, you find yourself entangled in a toxic relationship with one. How did you end up here? After all, narcissists love no one else above themselves. You are looking for someone to love and cherish you as much as you love and cherish them, yet you end up with someone incapable of loving you or even recognizing you beyond a glance.

Why do we fall in love with narcissists? What is it about them, or ourselves, that makes this supposedly impossible connection possible? Someone who is too engrossed in their ideology of themselves should fundamentally be unattractive, yet here we are.

We live in a world where fantasy has been glorified, and everyone keeps chasing after something unreal at some point. At the back of your mind, you know what you seek, or what is before you is superficial a smokescreen, yet the allure of attaining the impossible is too strong, so you yield.

Take speed dating, for example. Many people have participated in one or more. How do you get to know someone by summarizing highlights of their life? Speed dating is one of the lamest things in as far as relationships are concerned, yet many people throng the venues in the hope that they can find someone to settle with.

In such a case, who is at fault? Is it the narcissist who presents their case as a well-to-do, accomplished, person of your dreams kind of partner, or the seeker who is impressed by, and accepts nothing short of what the narcissist says they are? However, speed dating is not our concern, but an attempt at highlighting how complicated relationships can be, especially in terms of needs assessment (Houser, Horan, & Furler, 2008).

Narcissists are desperate, not just for attention, but also for self-love. They need to convince themselves that they are good enough constantly. If they are good enough for themselves, they have to be good enough for you too. This is one of the reasons why rejection doesn't always work well for a narcissist. It is not easy for them to reconcile it in their minds that someone thinks and feels they are not good enough.

While narcissists are at fault for their grandiose perception of themselves, at times you have to look inwards to understand your role in some unfortunate events. For the record, this is not to blame the victim, but to help you see things from a different perspective. Narcissists might be held accountable for manipulating you into a relationship, but you can get out. You deserve to be happy, and you deserve a happy and healthy relationship. Earlier on we saw some of the defining characteristics and manipulative traits of narcissists. This helped us understand who they are, how to identify them, and why they behave the way they do. We will try to understand you, the victim, and how narcissism is perpetuated in your life.

Why Am I Attracting Narcissists?

Ever felt like you are a narcissist magnet? Somehow, you keep ending up in relationships with narcissists, and this is not just about personal relationships, but the whole spectrum, including professional relations. While you might worry about attracting narcissists, this is not the main problem. The real problem is that you are holding onto them.

Let's try an exercise. Answer the following questions about your interactions and relationships truthfully:

- Do you have defined boundaries about behavior and attitudes you can tolerate from your partner?
- Would you end a relationship because your partner is selfish and doesn't consider your needs?
- How do you handle an abusive relationship? Walk away or stay and hope your partner will change?
- Do you excuse ill behavior from your partner and make excuses for them?

These might seem like mundane things, but they form the platform upon which a narcissistic partner will get away with devaluing you and your opinion all the time.

Here are some reasons why you might find yourself in a relationship with a narcissist, an abusive relationship you struggle to get out of:

Caregiving Spirit

Caregiving is a good deed. You empathize with someone who lacks, and out of the kindness of your heart, you take care of them. Many high achievers in society are in relationships with narcissists, some without knowing it. As a high achiever, you know you can take care of yourself. As a result, you always turn down the chance for someone to take care of you. You offer to pay for meals and drinks all the time. There is nothing wrong with taking care of yourself. However, to compensate for this lack of vulnerability, it is easier for you to take care of others. In so doing, you end up attracting peoplewho constantly need help.

You Fall for the Name-Dropping Charm

Everyone knows someone important. When it comes to celebrity stories, everyone has something that can light up a conversation. Whether it is true or another story, they heard from someone else; they tell their tales so vividly you can almost live in the moment through their words.

"Oh, you know Vettel too? He's such a nice person. He's friends with one of my buddies at work; we hang out from time to time."

If this kind of thing works for you, there is a good chance you will never see beyond a narcissist's name-dropping charm. Their stories and encounters are full of big names. It gets worse when they realize these appeals to you. They do this in a bid to conceal their insecurities about themselves and instead, lavish you with the idea of this glamorous life they live. Be warned, however, this charm is ingenuine. It is a ploy to seek and maintain attention. After all, who doesn't want to hear more about how to sneak into Buckingham Palace?

Flattery Is Your Undoing

Flattery can make you feel so good, but it doesn't last. At best, it can get you in a good mood. Narcissists crave attention. Nothing stands in their way when they want it. The use of flattery works for them because they can flatter you to get your attention, then immediately go on about them.

Flattery for a narcissist is not necessarily about needing compliments. In some cases, it is about paranoia, as the narcissist goes through their regular attention-seeking routine, and to boost their fragile ego.

Hovering for a Second Chance

If you are in a relationship with a narcissist and you break up with them, please let them go. Don't hold on, hoping that they might change and come back better. Narcissists love to hover around in the aftermath of a breakup. They had all your attention, which they don't enjoy anymore. This makes them feel helpless and abandoned, in which case the only alternative is to lure you back by any means necessary.

There are several tricks that they can use for this, including making a half-hearted apology, convincing you that they will not do what made you break up again, and so forth. Some will even send you photos of themselves looking sad. All this is to guilt you into taking them back.

Remember that you let them go because they disrespected you, and you felt that they cannot change. Such a person cannot change in a few days. They can, however, learn how to camouflage their real intent. Most people who take their narcissistic partners back usually suffer more pain and emotional trauma than they did earlier on.

You Sustain the Drama

Narcissists get bolder over time. They come at your boundaries, hoping you will cave and get softer with them. Your life with them is full of so much drama; you can't seem to catch a break. Netflix would be jealous of your life. Think about this for a moment: how peaceful is your life when your narcissist partner is out of town for work, or when they have traveled for some other reason?

When you are all alone, things are easy, smooth, peaceful, until they come back and all the upheaval starts. A narcissist will always leave you devoid of energy. All their demands will leave you worn, drained, and exhausted. All you ever do is provide for everything they need, from attention to affection. At the beginning of your relationship, this might feel okay, because perhaps you are trying to impress them or keep up with their energy. However, after a while, you realize you cannot keep up, and you are demoralized after an encounter with them.

You Are a Hopeless Empath

If there is one category that narcissists love and are surprisingly more drawn to it, it has to be empaths. Life can be very cruel and unfair. Why do such nice, loving, and caring people end up with partners who leave them more worn out than confidential documents having passed through a paper shredder?

The secret lies in your personality. As an empath, you are an understanding person. You believe that everyone deserves a chance. You see the good in everyone, even when you shouldn't. You believe that given time, you can turn a bad person into a good person. If you spend enough time with them, you can show them the goodness of their hearts, and make them change and embrace a new life (Stadler, 2017). This is where you go wrong, and open your life to toxicity.

Narcissists are wounded animals. As an empath, you want to take care of them. They know this better than you do. They know you are naturally inclined to try and fix them. When you meet, they will talk about how rough life has been for them in the past, perhaps in relationships, or their work, or anything else that draws your sympathy. While it is okay to be kind, you must be very careful about whom you show your kindness to.

Why Empaths Attract Narcissists

The attraction between an empath and a narcissist is one of those instinctive connections that just happen. You feel like you were meant to be together. You clickedthe very first time you met, and it seems you have foundthe right person for you until you wake up from the bad dream that has been months or years of your life. What's unfortunate for most empaths is that they will often end up in another relationship with another narcissist.

Narcissist-empath relationships are very toxic. You are exposed to so much pain that people who were once close to you can barely recognize you. Narcissists and empaths share some attributes that are attractive to one another, which is one of the reasons why they always seem destined to meet one another.

For the empath, however, it is nothing but bad news. All your goodness will be misconstrued for weakness and exploited by a narcissistic partner. In order to understand why this relationship happens in the first place, here are some reasons why you are drawn together:

You Are a Natural Healer

A narcissist will always appeal to an empath because you have natural healer tendencies. There is something so nurturing about you. Everyone knows it and it shows. You are a natural healer because you are sensitive. You are sensitive to people's feelings and needs.

Chapter 16: Brainwashing

What Is Brainwashing?

In the early 1950s, Brainwashing was coined by journalist Edward Hunter, who wanted to describe the Chinese Communists' efforts to control the minds and to think processes of the Chinese people after their takeover in 1949. Brainwashing is a method of controlling or influencing the personal beliefs, thoughts, attitudes, or actions of people themselves to make them believe what they had previously consideredto be false. The word "brainwashing" originated from its Nao, the Chinese term which means "washing the brain." Brainwashing is a method by which a person or group makes use of strict austerity measures to influence others to the will of the manipulator. But where does he stop honest persuasion and start brainwashing? Today, there are many forms of persuasion employed, especially in politics. For instance, a simple way to persuade a crowd to follow your instructions is first to state a few things that cause a' yes' response, then add items that are actual realities, and finally, recommend what you want them to do.

Methods

In psychology, the brainwashing study often referred to as the reform of thought, falls into the "social influence" sphere. Every minute of every day, social influence happens. It's the set of ways people can change the perceptions, values, and actions of other people. The enforcement approach, for example, attempts to bring about a change in a person's behavior and is not concerned about his ethics or values. It is the strategy of "Just do this."

Techniques That Are Used in Brainwashing

Isolation

Typically, the first tactic used in brainwashing is to isolate the victim away from his friends and family. They don't have to worry about any third party coming in and questioning what's happening.

Chanting and Singing

Chanting mantras is an essential feature of many religions, notably Buddhism and Hinduism, and nearly every church has some form of hymn-singing adoration. As each church member chants or sings the same words, their voices merge into one song, creating a strong sense of unity and collective identity. That, along with established singing effects such as lowered heart rate and relaxation, could cast the experience of community worship into a positive light. Increased suggestibility is a feature of such a state, and failure to maintain the trance is often followed by the punishment inflicted on cults, ensuring continuous enforcement of ultra-conformist behavior. They added that continuous lectures, singing, and chanting are used by most cults to alter consciousness.

Love Bombing

Cults want to reinforce the feeling that the outside world is threatening and gravely mistaken. In comparison, they also use "love bombing" to make themselves look accommodating. Love bombing means showering with lavish new or prospective hires and displaying attention and affection. The term has probably originated with either the Children of God or the Church of Unification, but can now be practiced in several different organizations. It is a phenomenon of social psychology that we feel strongly compelled to reciprocate other people's kind acts and kindness. It is, so the counterfeit affection, encouragement, and goodwill shown towards initiates by existing cult members are processed to create a growing sense of debt, obligation, and guilt. Margaret Singer called this an essential character of the cult, useful because it's precisely companionship and validation that many new cult recruits are searching for.

The psychologist Edgar Schein claims that people are triggered into a cult through a process of "unfreezing and refreezing. A new cult member starts to reject his old view of the world during the unfreezing stage and becomes open to the ideas of the cults. The cult solidifies this new perspective during refreezing. Schein mentions to love bombing as a critical point of refreezing—recruits who accept the philosophy of cults are rewarded with hugs and compliments but shunned when they ask too many skeptic questions.

Barratrous Abuse

Most cults hire attorneys to prosecute anyone who criticizes them publicly, no matter how trivial the criticism may be. Of course, the cult can usually afford to lose the lawsuits, while ex-cult members are often insolvent after giving the organization's life. Consequently, many ex-cultists are unable to mount an effective legal counterattack. Moreover, due to the ever-present threat of legal action, mainstream journalists are afraid to criticize cult or reference religious material.

Fatigue and Sleep Deprivation

Amway, a multi-level marketing company, has been charged with depriving its distributors of sleep during weekend-long events. It happened because they were including non-stop seminars lasting until the early morning hours, with only brief interludes during which musicians play loud music with lights flashing. A cultivation strategy that is sometimes used in combination with sleep deprivation includes advising participants to adopt special diets that contain low protein levels and other essential nutrients. As a result, the members of the cults will always feel tired, making them powerless to resist the dictates of religious doctrine.

Activity Pedagogy

How does a teacher motivate their students to follow ethical behavior and conformism? The solution is often to integrate some sort of physical exercise or sport into their teaching. Involved in jumping on the spot or running around, and consequently tired, children are less likely to argue or cause trouble. By acknowledging this phenomenon, several cults aimed to have members occupied as a means of control with an endless series of tiring activities. What distinguishes activity pedagogy from mere sports is that the increased mood and group identity experienced after physical activity will be used by a regime or cult to introduce ideological views that could otherwise be met with skepticism. Fatigue by exercise is yet another manner in which the barriers of people can be worn away as a means to enable them to embrace dubious ideas.

Lifton's Process

Robert Jay Lifton, the psychologist, studied former Korean War prisoners and Chinese war camps in the late 1950s. He determined that they would have undergone a multi-stage process that started with attacks on the sense of self of the prisoner and ended with what appeared to be a change of beliefs. Finally, Lifton defined a set of steps involved in the cases of brainwashing which he studied:

Assault on Identity

You're not who you think you believe you are. It is a deliberate assault on the sense of self of a target (also called its identity or ego) and its core system of beliefs. The agent hides everything that makes the target that he is: "You're not a soldier." "You're not a man." You're not protecting freedom. "For days, weeks, or months, the target is under constant attack to the point of becoming exhausted, confused, and disorientated. His convictions in this state appear less reliable.

Guilt

You are wrong. Whereas the existential crisis is setting in, the agent generates at the same time an intense sense of guilt within the target. He attacks the subject repeatedly and ruthlessly for any "sin" committed, big or small, by the target individual. For everything from the wrongness of his beliefs to the style he eats too slowly, he can criticize the target. The goal starts feeling a general sense of shame that all he does is wrong.

Self-Betrayal

Please agree with me you're awful. Once the subject becomes disoriented and submerged in shame, the agent pressures him to condemn his family members, friends, and peers who share the same "wrong" belief system that he maintains (either with the threat of physical damage or of continued mental attack). This abuse of his convictions and of those he feels responsible for heightening the guilt and lack of idea.

Leniency

I can help. The agent gives a small kindness or relief from the violence with the target in a state of crisis. He may offer a drink of water to the target, or take a moment to ask the target what he misses over the home.

Compulsion to Confession

You can help yourself. The target is faced with the comparison between the guilt and pain of identity assault. Then the sudden relief of leniency, for the first time in the brainwashing process, comes. The target may feel a desire to return the favor to the kindness that is shown to him, and then the agent may present the possibility of confession as a means of relieving guilt and suffering.

Challenging of Guilt

It is the reason because you are in pain. After some months of assault, confusion, breakdown, and leniency moments, the guilt of the target has lost all meaning—he's not sure what he's done is illegal, only knows he's wrong. It provides something of a blank slate that allows the agent to fill in the blanks: to whatever he wants, and he can add the remorse, that feeling of "wrongness." The agent attaches the guilt of the target to the creed system, which the agent attempts to replace. The goal comes to believe that the source of his guilt is his belief system.

That's not me; that's my attitude. The battled person is relieved to learn that there's an exogenous shock of his wrongness, that it's not himself who's intractably bad—that means he can escape his wrongness by running away from the corrupt system of beliefs. Then he can criticize the people and institutions associated with that system of ideas, and he will no longer be in pain. The goal can free itself from guilt by confessing to actions connected with its old policy of belief. The goal has completed its psychological rejection of its former identity with its full confessions. Now it is up to the agent to offer a new one for the target.

Self-Rebuilding

Progress and Harmony

The agent introduces a new belief system as the path to "good" if you want. At this stage, the agent stops the misuse, providing the target physical comfort and mental calm in combination with the new system of belief. The goal is made to feel it's he who has to choose between old and new, giving the goal the impression that his future is in his own hands. The goal has already abandoned his old belief system in reaction to leniency and abnormality. The choice is not a hard one: the new identity is safe and desirable because it is nothing like the one that has led to its breakdown.

Final Confession and Rebirth

I pick good. The target contrasts the agony of the old with the peace of the new. Then the target individual chooses a new identity, clinging to it as a preserver of life. He rejects his old system of beliefs and promises loyalty to the new one that will make his life better.

There are frequent rituals or ceremonies at this final stage to induce the converted target into its new community. Some brainwashing victims have described this stage as a sensation of "rebirth."

Because Lifton and other psychologists have described variations in what seems to be a distinct series of steps leading to a deep state of suggestibility, an interesting question is why some people end up brainwashed, and others don't.

Chapter 17: Covert Hypnosis

This process is also called conversational hypnosis or sleight of mouth. This term is mostly used by advocates of neuro-linguistic programming (NLP). NLP is a pseudoscientific approach to communication and interaction.

The technique's prime objective is to change the person's behavior subconsciously in such a way that the target believes that he changed his mind using his own will. The success of this process lies significantly in the fact that the remains unaware that he was hypnotized or that anything unusual occurred. The focus and attention of the subject are imperative during the conduct of

"Standard" hypnosis. This process is identical to salespeople talking to customers when they are tired. This is because critical thinking and questioning of statements require mental effort. The theme of "covert hypnosis" lies in approaching the subject when he is mentally and physically worn out. Covert hypnosis, irrespective of the fact, remains hypnosis. The element of fatigue is incorporated to make the critical thinking process more cumbersome.

Techniques

The notable trait of this process is that the hypnotized individual ultimately engages in hypnotic phenomena in an incognizant manner. There is a striking similarity between Covert hypnosis and "Ericksonian Hypnosis" in that both techniques work to reach deeper levels of consciousness operates by employing covert and subtle means. The surface structure of language then touches these more profound levels of consciousness. During covert hypnosis, the hypnotist controls another individual's behavior through establishing.

The subject feels a psychological connection with the hypnotist as he listens to him. The hypnotist, while displaying confidence and control, presents linguistic data in the form of metaphor:

However, it consequently helps in enabling a recovered deep structure of meaning that is directly relevant to the listener.

Put in another way, this process first builds unconscious states within the listener and then connects those states through covert conditioning. This is achieved, for instance, by shifting the use of time and use of identity in language.

An example:

The hypnotist may try to achieve a state of forgetfulness in the subject. This is done when the hypnotist talks with the subject of his feeling in that particular state in order to gain maximum knowledge about the subject. When the hypnotist discovers that this state is at its heightened peak, he can start talking about that state after this state has attained its maximum peak. That response will be contingent upon the fact that the suggestions were made to draw an immediate effect, and the reader was suggestible enough to be influenced in this way. The core objective of covert hypnosis is to shut down or at least minimize the analytical part of the subject's brain, lest he suspect something. All this may be achieved relatively quickly by an experienced practitioner.

Covert Hypnosis and Media

Real estate expert Glenn Twiddle in June 2010 appeared on the Australian television show A Current Affair. The segment reveals how he teaches real estate agents how to use these tactics on potential property buyers.

Covert Hypnosis in Fiction

Covert hypnosis has been portrayed in television series such as The Mentalist, although somewhat over-represented, the most prominent portrayal of covert hypnosis was in the "Russet Potatoes" episode in which a suspect uses covert hypnosis to manipulate characters in the episode and attempts to kill her boss. Another example of covert hypnosis was in the X-Files, where a man with a tumor in his brain is learning additional hypnosis abilities and using them to escape police captivity.

Learning Covert Hypnosis

If you want to learn covert hypnosis, first, you have to realize that it takes a long time to master properly, but if you practice every day, you will continually see positive results.

When learning how to do covert hypnosis, the difficulty for most people is not their inability to apply the methods, but rather their impatience and ignorance of how covert hypnosis is first and foremost.

There are extremely useful tips given below that will help you learn covert hypnosis.

Get into the Right Learning Mind Frame

It involves understanding how it takes dedication and persistence to master covert hypnosis. When you start learning covert hypnosis first, do not think it's going to be easy.

Covert hypnosis is all about knowing how the human mind functions and discovering how to interact effectively, mentally, and physically, with someone's mind in a subtle way.

While you can learn and apply such methods effectively within a very short space of time, you will not be able to do this effectively to different people without understanding the full processes leading up to that point.

Build Rapport

Many people make mistakes while establishing rapport. Relationship building involves creating a secure connection between the hypnotist and the subject of the hypnotist. The stronger the bond, the more powerful the technique of covert hypnosis is.

The partnership is more than what exists out there. It is an emotional and intense friendship, where people can be inside the minds of each other.

This hypnotic relationship bond is so strong that the subject will see the hypnotist as a figure of authority, and will be more than willing to do what the hypnotist wants them to do with little or no resistance.

Look for Trance Signals

Widening the social awareness networks by increasing the senses is of fundamental importance. It is construed as a critical step as it helps you to see the signs the subject gives as they enter a hypnotic trance.

Recognizing sure trance signs ensures you can move to the next stage of your technique of covert hypnosis.

Recognizing when someone is not hypnotically reacting to you is just as crucial because then you will realize that your manipulation is not working and that you have to find another process.

Understand Hypnotic Language

There is another name for Covert hypnosis, that is, conversational hypnosis, and you need to learn how to practice and sharpen your language skills to make it more hypnotic to influence a conversation.

Whenever you decide and manage to converse in a hypnotic language, it will cause the mind of the subject into a hypnotic state, which you can then influence to respond to in some hypnotic ways.

There is a range of primary and advanced methods in the hypnotic language, and you can do to achieve the hypnotic state of mind, from emotional triggers to manipulating someone's emotions to hypnotic storytelling.

What Hypnosis Is and Is Not

It is essential that you clear from the outset any doubts you have about hypnosis. Hypnosis is presented in the media as a means of total control over another person, and this enormous misconception has affected many people.

Any form of hypnosis won't give anybody complete control over the mind of another. This is just not possible.

Advantages of Covert or Conversational Hypnosis

You are directly influenced by the level of happiness and success of others. If you discover the fundamental secrets of ethical power, the world will be at your feet.

If you don't, you could end up living a quiet, lonely life, just like 95 percent of people who suffer from all kinds of problems needlessly.

Their suggestions and advice do not get much attention. They don't get their due respect. They lose clients and customers, and don't know why!

They are unable to communicate with confidence and have difficulty expressing their proposals to their colleagues. When they meet strangers, they lose their composure and make a poor initial impression.

They cannot get their children to listen and are usually discouraged because things don't seem to be going their way.

But it does get worse!

This is because no one tells you how to be as successful as you grow up. You've just picked up a few things here and there.

Covert Hypnosis Is a Simple Way to Convince People

Another big problem is conventional communications, and it doesn't work out by mere sales training.

You'll see people run away from you if they find you using such techniques.

There's a plethora of proof to suggest hypnosis might just be the answer you've been waiting for. The best part is the right kind of trance, which even works every day during routine interactions. That's okay. If you are talking to someone at a grocery store, at the post office, or elsewhere, you can successfully induce a trance in them. Conversational hypnosis is the technical term for this type of hypnosis.

It is the most potent way of influencing the human mind positively. Over the past 65 years, scientific research has shown that hypnosis can be used secretly. You can create ideas in the minds of people when communicating with them. They are not even going to know it's happening.

Neuro-scientific experiments suggest that all learning behavior and change unconsciously take place in the beginning. Afterward, the conscious mind catches up. So, if you want to be more successful, you've got to reach the people in their unconscious state. This is where the magic transpires.

Hypnosis offers the fastest way to tap into the unconscious mind! Research in the field shows the secret to persuasion is not to try to change people's minds, but to alter their attitudes first. For instance, you must first get somebody in the right mood. Only then can you change their perception and ability to agree with your point of view successfully.

Doctors, psychiatrists, and hypnotherapists have found that: hypnosis opens the mind to suggestion to the point that "normal" mechanisms in the brain can be overridden. At the unconscious level, it works profoundly to create near-instant shifts in hypnotic subjects.

The problem is that regular hypnosis is not possible. You can't walk around, holding a pocket watch, asking people to "look deep into my eyes." Traditional forms of hypnosis are best suited to clinical circumstances. However, you absolutely cannot apply any sort of hypnosis in everyday interactions. If you tried, at best, you will look foolish and outrage people at worst.

The conversational or implicit hypnosis is therefore suitable for typical situations. You can actually hypnotize someone who unintentionally asks for your assistance when chatting over a cup of coffee with them. Covert or conversational hypnosis:

- Is easy to learn, ethical to use, and enjoyable when you perform every interaction.
- Melts vital conscious mind resistance and makes way for easier and faster hypnosis.
- Participants simply don't know they're being hypnotized.
- Activates the suggestibility core of the brain so those thoughts sink into the unconscious mind and take root instantly.
- Creates an atmosphere for bringing someone else in.

Research-Based Evidence on Use and Utility

Since the early 1950s, the American Medical Association has allowed doctors to use hypnosis.

Covert Hypnosis Explained

Covert hypnosis can take many forms. It can be used as a pure and simple form of self-hypnosis, or it may be used to hypnotize another person or group of people.

Whether you choose to hypnotize yourself or another by using conversational hypnotism, the first step you'll want to take is to bring yourself in the desired state.

Getting Ready for Covert Hypnosis

You do not need to learn how to do hypnosis for yourself. Just relax by taking a few deep breaths in through your mouth and letting them out through your nose slowly and gently.

Chapter 18: How to Use Dark Psychology to Succeed at Work

The main reason many people want to learn about dark psychology is that they want to do better in their careers. They aren't content working the job they already have: they want to prove themselves to be capable of more.

But somewhere along the way, we figure out the truth: that getting ahead in our careers isn't necessarily a matter of skill, but of manipulation and persuasion. As you know, dark psychology is the best and most legitimate way to learn these skills, and now it's time to learn how to use them specifically in a work setting.

We have to think harder about how we interact with our co-workers. For instance, let's say we have a female early 20-something analyst in the midst of a post- graduation down-cycle who has encountered many challenges both professionally and personally since starting work a few years ago.

She frequently finds herself wanting to connect with people who are perceived to be more advanced in their careers or whose interests are different from her own. Being able to figure out why you are attracted to certain people is a valuable skill for early-career practitioners and likely contributes to her success as an analyst. If she wants to get ahead, she should follow along with all the directions in these pages, where we speak to dark psychology in the workplace directly.

Personality is an especially crucial subject for the context of the workplace because it is an environment where you have to interact with many different kinds of people, many of whom—you will soon find out—you don't actually know that well as people.

Dark psychology is broader than neurolinguistic programming, but NLP is where all of our tools and techniques of deep communication and manipulation come from. NLP is where the three big steps of manipulation and mind control originate from: establish your own state control and perceptual sharpness, imitate the unconscious cues of communication of your subject so that they incorporate you into their mind, and use one of the techniques.

People think constantly without even realizing it because most thought is unconscious. NLP is the way we take advantage of the unconscious nature of most thoughts to tell people's minds to change the structure before they even know it.

The topic of NLP is important for discussing personalities in the workplace because NLP has five main categories for the kinds of personalities people have. In the jargon of NLP, these "personalities" are actually called metaprograms. You would do well to identify the important people at your workplace within these metaprograms. Take advantage of your perceptual sharpness to ascertain this information.

As we have told you before, getting information about the subject is everything. But it is also true that our brains need to sort all the information we get into categories to understand the world better. These metaprograms do that job for you.

Metaprograms are more useful than personalities because they are more objective. They also focus on the motivations people have and the way they use logic, rather than on their mannerisms or less important patterns of behavior. Metaprograms do not simply describe how much you like attention or how nervous or relaxed you are—you may notice some aspects of each metaprogram that overlap with these traits, but metaprograms are much more specific than these less useful terms.

These NLP-styled personalities are not only a way for you to get more information about your co-workers. Remember the second step of NLP mind-reading and manipulation: you have to imitate the cues of communications the subject shows you. When you do this, you make them unconsciously see you as being like themselves. That means if you take on the traits of your co-worker's metaprogram, you make it easier for you to succeed in this step.

The last thing for you to know about metaprograms, in general, is that they are sorted in dichotomies. A dichotomy is a contrast between two items that are different. But while you should choose just one from each dichotomy in each metaprogram, you must remember that people are not as simple as being A or B. Any time we have a dichotomy—in any situation—picking one of the two is just a category you can use to simplify things and think of them differently. But you should not think of them as being always or exclusively one of the two. People are much more complex than this.

Our first metaprogram is between the dichotomy of options and procedures. People who are on the options metaprogram don't like being limited or being told what to do. They want as much freedom as possible, and they like to think about things from a general perspective rather than getting in the weeds. People on procedures, on the other hand, need to understand every small detail whenever they get into something new. Procedures people hate the feeling that there is something they are missing, and when detail is skipped, they fear they are missing something important.

The second metaprogram is external and internal. This metaprogram is concerned with people's incentives. External people want to be told by others when they do good work, and they want to be told when they do bad work, too. Internal people don't want to get outside opinions about their work, though. They feel they know when their work is good or not, and hearing what other people think is just a bother.

The third dichotomy in metaprograms is proactive and reactive. These metaprograms describe how someone deals with the future. Reactive people look at a calendar and are always thinking about how the work they are doing now fits into the picture of all of their work. This can be a hindrance because they think so much about planning ahead that they lose sight of what they are trying to do right now. Proactive people, on the other hand, hate thinking about the future or planning ahead. They only care about the here and now.

Our second-to-last is toward and away. This metaprogram is about goals and deterrents. All of us have things we look forward to in the future, but people are chiefly concerned about their goals, and they don't look behind them at all. Away people are the exact opposite of this. They can have issues looking ahead because they spend so much time thinking about what is behind them.

Finally, we have sameness and difference. Sameness people have a love for familiarity: they spend their time around things they already know. Things they don't know make them fearful, so these people avoid them at all costs. Difference people, on the other hand, are always craving new experiences to have, new people to meet, new foods to eat, and so on. If there is something they haven't experienced yet, different people want to experience it.

These are the five big dichotomies in metaprograms. Whoever the co-worker is who you want to use our dark psychology tricks on; you will want to sort them into these metaprograms. Now, when you use the Aristotelian technique of envisioning the future, you have a more objective stand-in for the person you will interact with.

You see, when we imagine someone in our heads, it isn't always accurate to how they really are. NLP's metaprograms are so useful because they make us think carefully about the kind of person our subject is.

Metaprograms are particularly good for the work environment because they force us to think about the people we work with more objectively. When you do Step 1 and prepare to get into the co-worker's mind with Step 2, you can use these metaprograms to paint a fuller picture of who you are going to use dark psychology on.

Since these are often just people we interact with exclusively in work environments, we can be surprised by how little we might know about them from a metaprogram standpoint. If you are being honest with yourself as you sort them into these dichotomies, you might realize you don't know very much about them at all. When this turns out to be the case, don't just go along with the dark psychology technique, anyway. There is no point in doing this when it won't work anyway—you can't adapt to the social cues of a person you don't even know yet.

That's why from here, you will have to do more intel-gathering on them first before you can even move on to Step 1. Step 1 can't successfully happen until you know the person and how they fit into all the metaprograms. Until you do that, you won't be able to properly imagine the interactions you have with them for Steps 2 and 3.

With that said, after you get to know the co-workers' metaprograms, let your senses do all the work in perceptual sharpness, use our exercises to prepare your state control, and imagine the interaction in your imagination, you are ready for Step 2.

For Steps 2 and 3, things go about the same when you are dealing with someone from your workplace. However, some techniques seem tailor-made for use in the work setting. We will go over these before moving onto our big lesson on neurolinguistic programming in psychology.

We will cover three big dark psychology techniques for the workplace before diving into the world of NLP. Social framing is a technique in which we paint a picture for the subject where adopting a certain behavior or idea will help them with social climbing.

Our social lives are one of the most important things to us as humans. That's why framing the truth about the subject's social environment is such a powerful tool for manipulating and mind-controlling people. As long as we make them believe they get a social reward for doing what we say, they will jump at the opportunity.

Executing this technique is simple. Assuming you have already mentally sorted them into the proper metaprograms, controlled your state, and are paying close attention to your senses.

Chapter 19: Knowing the Woman's Mind

Were you ever itching to get into the mind of a woman and ask what she is thinking exactly? But most people are motivated by the same fundamental motivations, as you are about to learn. When you know what they are, you can communicate with nearly every woman.

Also, if you haven't realized it, women are different from us. It's like they're from a whole other world sometimes, and they speak a different language. But it's not so difficult to understand people, and it's just different. Essentially, you need to understand the two primary ways women think differently from us.

How women get their way does not influence others in the same way that men do. We can't. They can't. We are less vulnerable than we are physically, and that is why most people (and some women) believe that they can easily overcome a woman through bullying. If a woman wants to get her way, she has to use other tools. The most common is the manipulation of the emotions of people.

She is a grown woman, and her emotions are controlled by her. However, men are real suckers for drama because they think they take responsibility for the emotional states of a woman.

When you think about it, it's hilarious. A woman can overwhelm a man with drama, literally. And who can blame them for this? For a very long time, it was their only choice. Not only physically are they weaker, but they have disadvantaged of authority for thousands of years and are compelled to use further creative ways to show men's strength. And of course, you've noticed that they've made it a science.

Let's clarify something before we go on: there is nothing wrong with the use of drama or manipulating people to do it. All of us use manipulation to obtain what we want. Some people refer to it as inspiration or influence. But we never force the person to respond to us, in any case.

In fact, men are more likely than drama to use bullying to get what they want. So it doesn't make sense to hate women to use the scene to get what they want. Instead, we will use this information to increase your choices for enhancing your relationships with women.

And that's just beginning to understand this: you will never find a woman who is "free of drama." People are emotional because it's a way to get what they want, what you have to do as a man is to learn how to handle the drama and prevent women from using it to dominate you. And believe it or not, this is precisely what women want of a man.

How Women Process Attraction

If this last statement puzzles you, it will clear the confusion to understand how women attract. This starts with understanding the one thing about women that most men have totally backward: what women want in a man. First, if you ask women for dating advice, that's right now because you'll just make yourself crazy. You might have worked this one out already.

Have you ever wondered why women don't seem to know what they want from a man's relationship? They say that they want a nice man who is good at treating a lady and who loves his wife. A sensitive man who opens the door to them asks them how beautiful they are and how wonderful a friend they are.

Instead; however, we are madly in love with people who are unrefined, crazy, cocky, a little childish, and who you just look at and wonder: "How the hell is this guy doing for him?" You are, in the meantime, the good-natured man who knows how to treat a lady and who loves his wife. A guy who is compassionate and caring and opens her door tells her how beautiful and kind she is.

And where do you get that? She slowly writes you out of her life as either a "great friend" or worse.

What's that all about in the world? You were the guy she said she needed. Why did you get to the place of your wife after watching her fall over her head for that "other jerk??" That's because what the women want is not what they think they want. And the sooner you recognize this, the sooner you will quit trapped in the' Friends' Corridor.' Now you shouldn't be shocked. After all, almost everyone does not claim that they want things that are entirely different from what their behavior reflects?

How many (men and women) do you know who is healthy, but who is consuming sugar-filled sweets, unhealthy fats, salt, and preservatives? How many people do you know who are wealthy, but who spend their money carelessly and who can't wait to go home to see TV throughout the day? This is because, while people want to be wealthy and safe, they are motivated by deeper motivations that most people don't take time to comprehend.

Don't tell people to judge. Many people are quite naive about the real reasons behind their actions, so they genuinely believe themselves when they tell you what they want. Yet look at their actions, if you want to know the real story.

Don't listen to what she says, if you want to know what women find attractive to look at her actions. Believe it or not, there's something "jerk" that most women like a flame moth.

They're making women feel safe and exciting.

This is an enticing mix because security andanticipation are two of the primary emotional needs people are looking for in romantic relations. If a man meets those two emotional requirements of a woman, he ignites a powerful unconscious attraction that transcends the reasoning mind of a woman.

Sound difficult to believe? Only think of how men you know who have given up thinking because of a woman's physical appeal. Think of how many people give up their thought and eat food they consider to be bad because they taste good. Think of how many people know who is spending their money on things which they don't need and end up having broken and then buy lottery tickets as "they want to be rich." This is why "jerks" (we will call them Bad boys) spark unconscious causes of attraction that seem to contradict a woman's spoken desires.

How's that?

First, these "bad boys" are immune to drama control, making them unpredictable… which are exciting for women.

Think about that, how exciting is it to a woman when a man answers her with what he wants because he is afraid to make her feel sad, frustrated, jealous, angry, unsure, stupid, or some other dramatic emotional state?

It's pretty dull, as you can imagine. The more beautiful a woman is, the more acquainted she is with people who bow to her every time she uses drama to dominate them. And frankly, she's all right with most people because it gives her more power. She just doesn't date such men.

She dates the people who are able to take over and who are not frightened by the drama. And that's where security and security are needed.

Think of this: how comfortable does a woman feel when she has a partner she can present? Does that mean he is insecure, weak, and obedient or reliable and trustworthy? Obviously, many women would like to have a nice man who knows how to treat the lady and who loves his wife. A caring, responsible man who opens her door tells her how beautiful and a great friend she is.

But most men are either: the nice man they say women want or the unrefined bad boy. Exceptionally few people could be both, and as the bad boy sees her need for security and excitement, she selects him above the boring man of beauty.

Chapter 20: Characteristics of Manipulative People

The main traits that are associated with manipulators and how they are able to control people around them. Moreover, we have focused on the ways in which personality traits that lean toward manipulation tend to manifest themselves in an individual. That's why we have gone into great depth in analyzing how and why the average manipulator acts the way they do.

On the whole, there is a debate whether being a manipulator is a question of in-born traits or whether it is a question of upbringing. In other words, we're referring to a nature vs. nurture debate. The fact is that there is no conclusive evidence linking specific genetic predisposition to acting in one manner or another. While traits such as psychopathy can be linked to actual physiological conditions in which the individual's brain may differ significantly, the fact of the matter is it is almost entirely an issue associated with upbringing.

For most folks, manipulative traits, such as the dark triad, are fomented in early childhood and adolescence. When kids and teens are subjected to certain types of experiences, they generally develop coping mechanisms that grow into the personality traits that we associate with manipulation. For instance, narcissism is generally linked to abandonment issues, which typically translate into a need for control. Of course, this isn't an iron law. But it does show that there is a clear correlation between the experiences that a child and teenager may go through, and how that translates into certain behavioral patterns down the road.

Therefore, it's important to analyze all aspects of a person's life in order to determine where one set of traits may emerge. It can be rather foolish to dismiss the effects of the environment on a person's behavior. In fact, many folks make a rash judgment in saying that manipulators, or even psychopaths, are just "born that way." The fact of the matter is that while there may be a physiological component (mental illness has been found to be a hereditary issue), most of the time, manipulative traits are the result of a certain set of experiences that a person goes through from an early age.

How Manipulators Select Their Victims

One of the most important things to consider in this discussion is how manipulators select their victims. A victim, by definition, is the recipient of the manipulator's actions. Therefore, the victim suffers negative consequences from the behavioral patterns exhibited by the manipulator.

On the whole, victim selection is generally random. This means that manipulators will simply sniff around, looking for someone they can take advantage of. When there is a greater amount of premeditation in the selection of a victim, then we might be dealing with a psychopath. As such, these individuals might make more careful study as to the type of person they seek to attack.

Nevertheless, most manipulators will simply seek out those who are closest to them. This is why family tends to be the first target on a manipulator's radar.

Generally speaking, manipulators look for weak individuals whom they feel won't be able to put up a fight. This means that for one reason or another, the victim is powerless to stop them. When you think of physical violence, this is one of the main criteria that goes into the selection of a victim.

On a deeper, more emotional level, manipulators will seek out people who stand to lose quite a bit more than the manipulator.

Think about that for a moment.

Let's go back to the example pertaining to the workers who must deal with a manipulative boss. In the end, the workers need the job far more than the boss does. If anything, the boss manipulates the employees more for personal pleasure than a logical business reason. Consequently, the workers are faced with a dilemma: they either put up with the manipulation or find another job.

The ultimate objective of the manipulator is to subdue their victims to the point where they will offer resistance to the manipulator's tactics. This means that the victim eventually becomes complicit in the manipulator's behavior. Sure, there are instances where the victim is unable to extricate themselves from the abusive situation they are in. In such cases, the victim can only hope to endure the situation until a time comes when they are able to get out finally.

Highly skilled manipulators will take the time to scout for potential victims. This occurs when a manipulator is able to identify the choice traits they are looking to find in their victims. As such, they will scout their surroundings and places they perceive will have the highest number of vulnerable individuals. That is why it's always a good idea to be skeptical of someone you don't really know in a place that you often go to. You never know who you might be dealing with.

Signs of a Manipulative Partner

One of the objectives on the mind of a manipulator might be to find a partner they can manipulate. This may occur either as a conscious behavior or an instinctive one. In the event of instinctive behavior, you can assume that the manipulator is not acting out of malice, but rather out of their own sheer desire. When you consider a conscious choice on the part of the manipulator, then you might actually be dealing with an evil individual who has a hidden agenda. So, it is important to recognize the warning signs before it is too late.

On the whole, manipulators can be easily spotted in romantic relationships by the subtle hints and lapses they show. For example, they appear to be sweet and attentive, but suddenly change and appear to be disconnected. You can tell this by seeing the way they pay attention to your conversation. Also, they might be very polite and caring but suddenly react abruptly when something that they don't like happens.

These are very subtle signs that you are dealing with someone who might not be entirely forthcoming. But the red flags get worse when you're dealing with someone who is jealous and possessive. This can begin with incessant text messages and calls. It's a progressive matter; they start off by increasing the number of calls and texts until you find that they are controlling everything you do. Eventually, they expect a tally and report of all the things you do.

In addition, a manipulative partner will strive to find out things that are negative, embarrassing, or even traumatic about your past. Then they will use that every time they can. For instance, a manipulator may use their partner's weight as a means of shaming. They will use this to coax their partner to comply; after all, "no one will love you as much as I do." These types of statements are a clear indication that there is a manipulation attempt.

These red flags are important to keep in mind as they can quickly degenerate into an abusive relationship. Highly skilled manipulators will make the transition so subtle that the victim won't even notice the relationship is degrading to that level. In the end, all the victim can feel is the effects of the abuse.

How to Know You Are Being Targeted

It can be hard to know if you are being targeted by a manipulator. Perhaps the easiest way to go about this is to confront the manipulator. If you happen to run into someone who is overly friendly, then this ought to be a red flag for you. Also, if you happen to be surrounded by people who only remember you every time they need something from you, then you know you're definitely being targeted.

Unless you know a person well, it's always a good rule of thumb to keep an eye out on everyone. While this may seem like paranoid behavior, the fact of the matter is if you are able to be alert, the chances of being nabbed by manipulators are rather slim.

Here are some practical tips:

- Be wary of overly friendly strangers.
- Watch for offers and deals that are "too good to be true."
- Keep an eye out for sudden mood swings.
- Watch out for contradicting behavior and words.
- Pay attention to the moment in which people approach you.
- Avoid responding to unsolicited advice.

These situations are all indicative of a manipulator trying to "test" you. If they find that you are responsive, then they may feel compelled to continue their advances until you give in to what they want. In the end, it's usually best to just get away from these people. You may never have to engage them openly; all you may have to do is just move away from them.

How to Deal with a Manipulator

If you happen to find yourself dealing with a manipulator, here are three very important steps that you can take to help you better deal with this type of individual.

Try your best to get away from the situation. While there are circumstances in which getting away from a manipulator may be virtually impossible, it is the most recommended course of action to get away from them as far as possible. This will take away their opportunities to manipulate you. Moreover, if you can completely extricate yourself from a situation (such as finding a new job), then the entire better.

Find out what they are using to manipulate you and then take it away from them. If you can identify what they are using against you, then you will be able to take that weapon away from them. In fact, you may even be able to use it against them. That will be a clear indicator of the manipulator that they can't have their way with you any longer.

Know your rights. If you happen to be in an abusive relationship or situation, you have the right to seek help. This can be any form of help that may be available to you, but you must act on it. If you know you are being affected by a manipulative and even abusive person, but fail to say anything about it, you may never get the help you need. So, it's important to speak up.

Avoid the blame game. Do not think for a second that this situation is your fault. Also, there is no need to blame the manipulator, even though they are responsible for their actions. When you play the blame game, you are hurting yourself by making it seem that you are directly, or indirectly, responsible for what's happened. So, even if you are the victim, it's not your fault that this has happened to you. By the same token, the manipulator is not at fault for being a manipulator. However, they are responsible for their actions.

Know when to quit. If you choose to confront the manipulator, you need to know when you may need to get away from them. There is only so much energy you can spend on a person like this. Oftentimes, dealing with a manipulator becomes a war of attrition. So, your determination to win that war may leave you more spent, both physically and emotionally, than what you stand to gain.

Chapter 21: Victims

Just as manipulators frequently share all sorts of similar traits and behaviors, they also share similar taste in victims. Manipulators, like all predators, look for the easiest targets that pose the best chance of success. Just as the pack of wolves will pick off the weakest members of a herd, the manipulator will look for people who they deem are emotionally easy targets, using a sort of natural sense for whom to go after. Because they go for these specific traits, they are usually incredibly efficient in what they do. Manipulators have essentially mastered the art of picking up the perfect target. Take alook at some of the most commonly targeted traits, as well as the signs someone around you may be being abused or manipulated.

Traits of a Victim

While some manipulators may go out of their way to target other types of people, the vast majority will go for ease of a target overlooking for a challenge. When they are going to manipulate others, they want to make sure they can get away with it, as well as to get away with any of the behaviors they wish to expose the other person too. Some manipulators never move beyond emotional exploitation, while others will go out of their way to work their ways up to physical or sexual abuse. Ultimately, these are some of the easily exploitable traits that manipulators everywhere look for:

Empathetic

The perfect manipulation victim is empathetic. When they are empathetic, they are far easier to manipulate. Think back to the reason's manipulators tend to manipulate—one is to get what they want. An empath is going to be quick to tune into whatever it is that the other person needs, and is much more likely to want to give whatever it is, whether it is attention, affection, or companionship. This makes the empath an ideal target.

Further, empaths, especially if they meet some of the other criteria on this list, are frequently quite forgiving. They will be quick to write off some bad behavior as a fluke or an unfortunate consequence of the circumstances, and they will be more likely to believe that the manipulator will not continue the behaviors. They are also more likely to fall for guilt trips, making manipulating them somewhat easier than others. What the empath offers most of all is the patience necessary to put up with the manipulator's antics.

Caregiver

People with caregiver personalities thrive upon taking care of others. They love to make sure those around them have their needs met. They naturally care about what others need and are often also quite empathetic. Because they feel fulfilled taking care of the needs of others, manipulators can typically twist things around to get whatever they want. The manipulator is quite skilled at convincing the caregiver that he needs something he does not, and the caregiver, wanting to make sure the manipulator is cared for, will do so.

Caregivers, in particular, tend to be quite patient—they are willing to put up with far more than necessary simply because they feel they can handle it. They are likely to forego ending a relationship they see as abusive or manipulative if they believe that the cause of that abuse or manipulation is old wounds within the manipulator that are causing the behaviors in the first place. Instead, the caregiver will put up with the manipulation while diligently attempting to fix the manipulator's problems.

Codependent

Codependency and caregiver personalities are incredibly similar—both the codependent and the caregiver will pour themselves into their relationship, hoping to fix the manipulator, but the codependent will wholly identify with the relationship. The codependent is more likely to put up with far worse manipulation and abuse simply because she feels she cannot move on from the manipulator. While she may recognize what is happening, she feels so intricately intertwined with the manipulator and that relationship that she feels there is no life without the manipulator. Her very identity will be wrapped up in caring for the manipulator, catering to his every whim, even to her detriment. Even though it will hurt her, she continues to do so anyway to a fault. Her codependent nature becomes a point of contention for her as the relationship that she feels is all that she is also hurting her. She may not like the way she is being treated, but she will want to continue to pour herself into the relationship.

Grew Up in Dysfunction

Those who grew up in the throes of dysfunction oftentimes have skewed ideas of what normal is. They see the way they grew up as normal and will oftentimes revert back to what is familiar to them, even if familiar is harmful. For these people, they may see no red flags with the manipulator's behaviors, particularly if manipulation was one of the key features of their own dysfunctional upbringing.

Since they grew up around unhealthy relationships, their own tolerance for abuse is usually quite extreme. They may be annoyed, but see it as unworthy of ending a relationship or friendship. Even things like physical abuse may not be deal-breakers for those who grew up around it and had such abuse normalized for them. This makes them particularly easy targets because they will be so tolerant and already desensitized to too much of the abuse and manipulation that the manipulator will be utilizing.

Low Self-Esteem

Perhaps one of the most attractive of traits to a manipulator when looking for a victim is low self-esteem. You will learn that breaking someone's self-esteem is oftentimes a core theme in much of the manipulation you will be learning about. Manipulators need people with low self-esteem because they will not fight back or make things difficult—instead, they will put up with the abuse and accept whatever is being said simply because they do not have the self-esteem to trust themselves.

Because the first active step in much of the manipulation is usually breaking down self-esteem, manipulators love shortcuts. Just as how a wolf will go for the weakest in a herd, the manipulator will go for theeasiest target, and frequently, those are the ones whose self-esteem is already so weak and shattered that they can do whatever they want with impunity.

Ultimately, the more of these traits that an individual has, the more attractive they are to the manipulator. With that in mind, if you feel like you see any of these signs in yourself, these are likely to be your weaknesses. If you know you have low self-esteem, for example, you should be aware of how that can work against you if you are not careful.

Signs of Abuse or Manipulation

Oftentimes, those who have been manipulated show very similar behavioral signs. After being victimized for so long, they pick up similar behavioral patterns in an attempt at self-preservation. Take a look at some of the most commonly exhibited signs and symptoms of manipulation.

Self-Sacrificing or Martyrdom

Those who have been manipulated enough oftentimes develop an attitude that they do not deserve to be taken care of. They see themselves as expendable, not worth the effort it would take to do things for themselves. Rather than focusing on bettering themselves, they focus on making sure the manipulator is cared for, just as the manipulator intended. They will oftentimes give up whatever they are asked to do, or volunteer to be the one missing out simply because they have been conditioned to do so.

Self-Sabotage

Oftentimes, the victim becomes so accustomed to not getting what he or she wants that they will begin to believe they are not deserving of having needs met. They are so used to being seen as expendable and with their needs as unimportant that they will begin to act as such as well. If they get something nice, they will believe that they do not deserve it, which can convince them that they should do something to sabotage what they have. For example, if someone has just gotten a new job that pays well, it is possible that he would decide that he does not deserve that job, and because he does not deserve that job, he would possibly perform poorly unconsciously, believing that he is not good enough anyway, so he has no point to bother trying.

Fiercely Protective of Abuser

People who are regularly exposed to abuse or manipulation frequently become fiercely defensive and protective of anyone they feel threatens them. Because the manipulator frequently convinces the victim that the victim is exceedingly lucky to have someone like the manipulator around, and intentionally manipulates the feelings of the other person in an attempt to trick the other person into falling in love, the victim often feels conflicting emotions when the manipulator is talked poorly about. Oftentimes, the victim will vehemently defend the manipulator to anyone who says something they disagree with, feeling the need to protect the manipulator.

Mental Health Issues

Through constant stress from the manipulator, it is not uncommon by any means for people to develop mental health issues. After extended periods of time being manipulated, belittled, and demeaned in order for the manipulator to gain a sense of control over the individual being manipulated, the victim is more prone to depressive and anxiety symptoms.

Being Distrustful

After time spent being demeaned and manipulated, people tend to grow to be quite distrustful. Especially once they have come to discover the truth and they understand that someone they had trusted actually was using them in some of the worst ways imaginable, they lose the capacity to trust easily and readily.

Fearful Behavior

Because people who are manipulated often find themselves getting to a point where they fear the reaction of the manipulator if they do not concede to whatever the manipulator wants, the victims tend to grow fearful in general. They are so used to someone taking advantage of the situation and making them feel bad about themselves when they are not living up to expectations that they often come to expect the worst from others as well. They grow timid and concerned with assuming that people around them have the worst intentions, and that leads to a fearful demeanor, especially when the victim perceives that he or she has failed in some way.

Paranoia

Typically, in a combination of becoming fearful and distrustful, those who are manipulated sometimes develop a paranoid view of the world. They worry that they are being taken advantage of, even when they are not, and they become inherently suspicious of those who do try to help, assuming there is some sort of ulterior motive at play when someone does offer help. For example, if a manipulation victim is asked if she wants help with studying for an upcoming exam, she may wonder what the other person wants in return, even if the other person is simply doing it out of kindness or a genuine interest in getting to know her better with no strings attached.

Chapter 22: Deception

Deception is going to refer to the act, whether it is kind or cruel or big or small, or causing someone to believe that something else is untrue. Even those who consider themselves pretty honest are going to practice some of this deception, and there are several studies out there that show how the average person, no matter how good-hearted they think they are, are going to lie several times in a day.

When it comes to these lies, some of them are going to be big lies that are meant to cause harm and hide the bad that the liar has done. But for the most part, the liesthat we say are going to be small, usually white lies, thatare used to spare the feelings of another person or get us out of a situation that is making us uncomfortable.

You will find that deception is not always going to be an act that is outward. It is also true that people are going to tell lies to them. There are a lot of reasons that they would do this, such as trying to maintain a healthy dose of self-esteem to some serious delusions that are sometimes beyond their control. While it is sometimes seen as harmful to lie even to yourself, some experts are likely to argue that certain types could also have a positive effect on your overall well-being as well.

Researchers have long searched for ways to find out when they can tell whether someone is lying or not. The polygraph test, which is something that a lot of us already know about, has long been controversial, and it has long been known that some people are easily able to lie to the test and get away with it. This is especially true if the individual has some psychiatric disorder.

With this, we need to take a look at why people lie. No one likes to feel deceived about anything, and when anyone, especially a public figure, ends up being caught in a lie, it can turn into a big headache for them. But while a lot of us are going to pride ourselves on our scrupulous honesty, and we try to stay as far away as possible from those who are fine with falsehoods, the truth is that all of us have lied at one point or another.

Experts find that having a small amount of deception can be important when it comes to maintaining a society that is healthy and can function well. The formal study of deception was once the domain of theologians and ethicists, but in recent years, more psychologists have turned over to look at the reasons why people are going to lie, as well as some of the conditions that make people more likely to lie.

The Types of Deception

Deception is going to include a lot of different things, but often, it is going to include a type of communication or omission that will serve to omit or change up the whole truth from another person. This is done in a manner that benefits the deceiver. If they hide the truth or change up the facts a little bit, then their victim will believe what the deceiver wants, and the deceiver will win. This can sometimes be a little white lie that helps to protect the feelings of the victim, but more often than not, it is going to be done at the expense of the victim.

Examples of this kind of deception are going to range from false statements to claims that are misleading, where relevant information is taken out. This is done so that the victim is going to be led to a false conclusion. In some cases, we may think that this oil is going to benefit the health of our brain more than some other foods we would eat.

However, the amount of omega-3 fatty acids that are found in sunflower oil is going to be low. And thanks to the other ingredients found in the oil, it is usually not seen as something that is all that good for the health of your brain. So, while sunflower oil does have some omega-3 fatty acids, and those are good for your brain, the information is going to lead the victim to infer false information about just how beneficial the sunflower oil is for them.

When it comes to deception, we have to look at the intent of the deceiver. If they got the information wrong on accident and shared it with the victim, then this is not deception. But if the deceiver wants to make sure that the victim is getting the wrong information on purpose, then it is going to be deception. The intent is going to be vital because it is going to show us the difference between an honest mistake and deception.

A good thing to look at here is the Interpersonal Deception Theory. This theory is going to explore some of the interrelations that show up between the communicative context and the sender and receiver cognitions and the behaviors in the exchange.

Now, there are going to be a few different types of deception that can show up depending on the situation and what the deceiver is hoping to get out of the exchange. Some of the forms of deception that you can use or encounter in your life include:

Lies

This is when you will make up information or when the deceiver is going to give information that is opposite of the truth, or at least very different from the truth.

Equivocations

This is when the deceiver is going to make a contradictory, ambiguous, or indirect statement.

Concealments

This is when the deceiver is going to omit some important information or relevant to the given context, or they are going to engage in some behavior that will ensure that the relevant information is as hidden as possible.

Exaggerations

This is when there is a big overstatement, or the deceiver is going to stretch the truth as much as they canget away with.

Understatements

This one is going to head in the opposite direction. With this one, you are going to find that the deceiver is going to downplay the aspects of the truth as much as possible.

Untruthful

This is also going to be when the deceiver is going to try and misinterpret the truth a bit.

Many of us think that we are good at deception. However, this takes a lot of talent and work, and since most people are good at catching lies and deception, it is hard to pull off on someone.

Three main motives are focused often on when it comes to why people like to lie and deceive others. According to Buller and Burgoon (1996), there are three methods that you can use to distinguish deception based on that interpersonal deception theory from before. These include:

Identity

The deceiver may lie to save their self-image or to remain in the same position with others, or with that one person, as they did before.

Relational

This is the deception that is done to help maintain the bonds or the relationships that you have.

Instrumental

This is when the deceiver is going to lie because it helps them to protect their resources or avoid any punishment that they should receive.

Depending on who uses the deception, it can sometimes be easy to see. Many of us think that we are good at deceiving those around us when, in reality, we are not. We end up being caught, especially if we are close to the other person we are trying to deceive.

But some people are good at deceiving. They are so good at this that they can end up deceiving someone for many years or more, and the victim, as well as those around them sometimes, will never be any the wiser about it. This can be dangerous because often, we don't know what is being kept from us and what we should know about a particular situation.

Simulation

Simulation is going to be any time that the deceiver exhibits some false information. There are going to be three different techniques that can be used with this, including mimicry, fabrication, and distraction. Let's dive into each of these to see how they work.

The first method is mimicry. This is when you will copy another example or another model. For example, animals are going to use this to deceive their predators through auditory or visual means in most cases.

Then there is the idea of fabrication. This is when the other person is going to make up a brand-new lie or story that fits their needs. For the deceiver to make something appear to be something that it isn't, usually to encourage the other person to divert, endanger, or reveal the victim's resources, is going to be a fabrication. The deceiver wants to learn something from the other person, and they want to cause some harm to the victim. This means that they are going to tell a fabrication to completely throw the victim off guard and make it so that they aren't sure what to believe.

An excellent example of this would occur in World War II. During this time, it was common for the Allies to work with hollow tanks that they would make out of wood rather than the usual materials. This was done so that the German planes would think that a large unit of them was moving in on an area. In reality, the real tanks were hidden and were moving in the opposite direction towards their real target.

Distraction is the next simulation. This is when the manipulator is going to try and get someone's attention from the truth, usually with some bait, or something that they know will divert the attention away from whatever the deceiver is trying to hide. Bait and switch, as well as many of the fraud techniques that we hear about, are going to work with the idea of distraction as well.

How to Use Deception

Now that we have a better idea of what deception is all about, it is time to look at a few of the techniques that you can use to put deception to work for your own needs. It is often not considered ethical to use deception, even though most people are going to use it at one point or another to get what they want. Learning how to use deception properly can make it more likely that someone is going to do what you want.

Chapter 23: Distance in Communication

Focusing on the United States, there are four types of distances that people use to communicate on a face-to-face basis. These distances are intimate, personal distance, social distance, and public distance. Starting with the intimate distance, it is used for highly confidential exchanges as zero to two feet of space between two individuals marks this zone. An example of intimate distance includes two people hugging, standing side-by-side, or holding hands. Individuals with intimate distance share a unique level of comfort with one another. If one is not comfortable with someone approaching them in the intimate zone, he/she will experience a significant deal of social discomfort.

Firstly, personal distance is used for talking with family as well as close acquaintances. The personal distance can range from two to four feet. Akin to intimate distance, if a stranger walks into the personal zone, the one is likely to feel uneasy being in such proximity with the stranger.

Secondly, there is the social distance used in business exchanges or when meeting new people and interacting with groups of people. Compared to the other distances, social distance has a larger range in the range that it can incorporate. Its range is four to twelve feet, and it depends on the context. It is used among students, acquaintances, or co-workers. As expected, most participants in the social distance do not show physical contact with one another. Generally, people are likely to be very specific concerning the degree of social distance that is preferred, as some require more physicaldistance compared to others. In most cases, theindividual will adjust backward or forward to get the appropriate social distance necessary for socialinteractions.

Thirdly, we have public distance, which is twelve or more feet between individuals. An example of public distance is where two people sit on a bench in a public park. In most cases, the two people on a bench in a public park will sit at the farthest ends of each other to preserve the public space. Each of the earlier types of proximity will significantly influence an individual's perception of what is the appropriate type of distance in specific contexts. One of the factors that contribute to individual perceptions of how proxemics should be used is culture. Individuals from different cultures show different viewpoints on what the appropriate persona; space should be.

Fourthly, there is the concept of territoriality, where individuals tend to feel like they own and should control their personal areas. We are inclined to defend our personal space. When someone invades this personal space, then the individual will react negatively as it is an invasion of territory without express permission. At one point, you asked a stranger to keep some distance from you because you felt uncomfortable with the person standing close to you. Sometimes standing next to a person may also denote that you are creepy and may be intending to harm the person.

If one is talking to someone, the person violates your personal space, and you allow it, then it signals that you are okay to intimate ideas. Intimate ideas in this context include highly personal issues that one can talk about with another person. For instance, if you walk and sit close and in contact with a woman watching television and she approves of your behavior, then it is indicative that she is likely to allow you to have a personal talk that may be intimate in nature. Such discussion may include your health challenges or mental health and not necessarily sexual issues. For this reason, one should carefully weigh the need to invade the personal distance.

Regarding children, violating personal distance will make them freeze due to feeling uncomfortable. If a teacher sits next to a student or stands next to a student, then the student is likely to feel uneasy and nervous. However, they are instances where the invasion of personal space is allowed and seen as necessary. For instance, during interviews or when being examined by a doctor, invasion of private space by the person with an advantage is allowed. The panel during an interview may move or ask you to move closer, which may violate your personal space. A doctor may also stand closer to you, invading your personal space, but this is necessary due to the professional demand for their service.

As such, when one avoids personal distance, and the individual is expected to be within this space, then the individual may be feeling less confident or feeling ashamed. For instance, if a child has done something embarrassing, he or she is likely to sit or stand far from the parent during a conversation. For this reason, it appears that one should feel confident, assured, and appreciated to approach and remain in personal space when needed.

Additionally, staying in personal space during intense emotions may portray one as resilient, understanding, and bold. Think of two lovers or sibling quarreling, but each remains in the established personal space. The message that is being communicated is that the individual is confident that he or she can handle the intense emotions from the other person. For most people, they only allow their lover to stay in their personal distance when feeling upset because they trust that the person can handle the known behavior of the affected person. Since being in personal space places a person within physical striking range, most people will only allow trusted and familiar individuals into their personal space.

Equally important is that invasion of personal space is justified because it is a part of professional demands.

Think of a new teacher that is trying to help a student solve a mathematical equation. In this aspect, the teacher is a stranger because he or she is new to the school. By sitting or standing close to the student, the teacher is invading the personal space, but the established norms in this context allow the student not to feel unease. For emphasis, this case is not unique as it aligns with stated expectations that people will welcome known or unfamiliar people in their personal space only if they trust them and, in this case, the student feels safe with any teacher. For this reason, the operationalization of distance in communication is mediated and moderated by established culture.

In most cases, one can start with public distance before allowing the interaction to happen in a personal or social space. For instance, as a student during tournaments, you could have initiated non-verbal communication with the student from the other college before suddenly feeling connected to the individual and allowing him or her to move into personal space as a potential girlfriend or boyfriend. At first, the target person saw you as a stranger but allowed you to make non-verbal communication within the public space. When the person felt the need to connect more with you and have given you the benefit of the doubt, the person allowed you to move through public distance and social distance to enter their personal space.

For instance, a lot can be learned from studying distance and space in communication. Being allowed into the social and personal distances implies that the person trusts that you will not harm them emotionally and physically. For the intimate distance, being allowed into this distance implies that the person trusts you so much and is confident that you can never harm them and that you share a lot. For instance, a mother holding her baby close enough to her signals that the baby is feeling assured of security and protection. When two lovers move closer until their faces are almost touching suggests trust and confidence that the other person feels safe and protected.

Relatedly, if arguing with your child or lover and the individual moves farther from you physically, then it suggests that the person no longer feels safe with you being within their personal distance. Issues that can cause someone to expand the distance between you and them include the risk of violence from you and emotional issues. If you occasionally act violently, then chances are, your lover or children will expand the personal distance to social distance because this is where they feel safe due to your personality and character. It then appears that your prior behavior will also affect the distance during communication.

Nevertheless, they are other issues that cause individuals to extend the distance of interaction, and these include having a medical condition or having hygiene issues. For instance, if you are sweaty, then chances are that the other person may prefer to extend the distance of communication between you and them. Having oral hygiene issues may also make the other person move far away from you because the smell turns them off. For this reason, interpreting the distance between communicators should also include hygiene and health-related issues that impact this distance.

For instance, some medical conditions can make people maintain some distance from you or be closer to you physically. For instance, some conditions may attract uneasiness, and this includes epilepsy. People with epilepsy get seizures, and this can make people feel unease being closer to them because they inadvertently fall. On the other hand, having hearing issues or sore throat may make people move closer to you physically to facilitate effective communication. However, these are exceptions when analyzing space and distance as forms of non-verbal communication, but they should betaken into account where necessary.

In some cases, it is welcome to invade personal distance merely by the circumstances. For instance, when attending a match in a full packed stadium or sitting to watch a movie in a movie theater, one will have his personal invaded due to the sitting arrangements. In this context, one may feel uneasy with this arrangement, but he or she has little control over the situation. While we value and seek to protect personal spaces, some situations make us allowing the invasion of this space because it is beyond control.

Chapter 24: When "No" Means "Yes"

Have you ever rented a car and been adamant that you didn't want insurance, but somehow walked out with it, anyway? Have you wondered how they got you to believe that you needed something that you didn't want in the first place? There is a sort of power and control within the resounding no. The rental agent already knows that you are going to walk in telling them what you want and don't want. Most people do not want the extra insurance because they have their own insurance and feel like paying extra for more insurance isn't worth it, especially when you probably aren't going to need it. The resounding "no" is so common that it is something salespeople don't even pay attention to anymore. It is an instant reaction that is driven by the fear of getting swindled into doing something that you do not want. So, you walk in already with your mind made up.

However, the rental agent found a way to get you to buy the product still. Think about it, before they even work on your contract, they go outside and walk you around the cars. During this time, they ask you questions about your trip, what you need it for, and then they start telling you about the amenities of the car—that they carry car seats, and they sell you the coverage based on what appeals to you through the conversation you had. You felt like you had a great conversation with the salesperson, but in reality, they were using the time to prey on you because they know what you will need on this trip you are taking and how what they have to offer will alleviate your stress and/or solve your problem.

When changing your audiences' answer from no to yes, it is about understanding how they make decisions, what appeals to them—by testing the waters—how they remember things, and how they look into the future. Most of the time, people remember important dramatic experiences that turn out badly. The rental agent might ask you if you have car insurance and you tell them that you have what the law requires because you own your car.

This is when they realize that they want to protect their car, but they also want to make you think that they are protecting you from having to pay tons of money out of your pocket. So, they will tell you that they have rental coverage that covers the car bumper to bumper. It is only $11–$14 a day depending on the car size, and there is no deductible. If anything happens to the car, it will be covered, and you will just walk away without paying a dime. This might sound appealing to the customer, but they still feel like they don't need it. So, they tell the rental agent "no" again.

This is when the agent moves to a story to sway the customer. The agent tells the customer they understand how they feel. Telling them that they buy the coverage doesn't help. They need to tell them a story that they will remember, a dramatic one that will sway them to their side. The agent brings up an encounter with a previous customer who felt the same way as the current one. The customer was adamant about not getting the coverage that covered the car and rented the car without it.

Another car ended up hitting them in the parking lot, and they walked back in asking if they could get the coverage. The rental agent had to end the rental contract and not give them the coverage because it is illegal to sell it after the rental agreement has been made and after an accident. The customer ended up paying for the damages out of their pocket, as well as the life of the rental in the shop, which means they had to pay the amount of the rental up to five days. All because they didn't want to pay an extra $30. Due to this story, the current customer ended up purchasing the coveragethat covered the car.

When the agent was telling the story to the new customer, all they remembered was the outcome of the crash in the parking lot. They didn't remember anything else about the story, just that they didn't want to go through what the previous customer went through.

Covert Persuasion can be used in different situations, especially when you are trying to win and bring them over to your side. In customer service, you want them to talk about your competitor and discuss their past experiences because if they were satisfied with that experience, they wouldn't be talking to you. One of the things that you have to do is make sure that you don't scare them away so that they do not want to purchase from you.

Have them tell you a story of a great purchase experience they had. This helps you from not scaring them off because you are having them remember a fun experience. For instance, if you are a stockbroker and the potential customer is someone who has lost money in the stock market, you will understand why they don't want to risk money again. But isn't that the risk with the stock market? You're not going to make money every time.

The broker has to be careful in this situation, and they cannot guarantee the potential customer or investor that they will not lose money again. That will be a lie, and that will break their trust right there. The broker has to point out that it is a possibility that they would lose money again. However, it is more likely that they will get typical returns with their investment.

Persuasion research is very clear, especially with covert persuasion. The speaker must show the audience both possible outcomes for them to be successful. If the speaker doesn't indicate that the investor might lose money in the stock market, they will continue to be afraid of it and choose not to invest with your brokerage firm.

When you show them that losing money is a possibility, you also show them what else could happen within reason. If you make it sound too good to be true, the possible investor will feel like they are being manipulated, and they will still choose not to go with your firm's offer. By keeping it realistic, there is a high chance that they will succumb to your persuasions.

Be clear with your message delivery. If the possible investor lost the first half of the game, they need to come in strong during the second half. Never let what happened in the past determine what they could possibly achieve in the future.

The whole idea of persuading people is to take away their fear of saying yes, which is normal. People tend to have a fear of the unknown and how their life will change. If you are trying to help someone quit smoking, the person will resist at first because the fear of deterring from their normal routine is too much for them. To help them overcome this fear, you will have to substitute their current fear with one that is far worse. Basically, you are scaring them beyond their worst fears. For instance, the speaker tells the person that if they continue to keep smoking every day that it is going to cause you to die. Can you imagine your kids and grandkids standing over your casket? They will remember you the way you looked in that casket. The idea of their family looking over their dead body scares them, especially when it is something that they could have prevented. This is when the speaker makes the fear less painful by helping them cut down. Tell them to start small by cutting down to half a pack a day this month, then only one every day next month and by the next month, you don't need them anymore. Wouldn't it be great to show your family that you don't need to smoke? Wouldn't it be great to show them how healthy you are?

The speaker used fear to persuade the person to stop smoking and then gave them a set of instructions that will help them with the new decision that they made. The person was able to see how changing their life and going with what you wanted wasn't hard if they worked at it. They weren't going to be worse off because of the decision, but better.

So, once the speaker can change or is persuaded to do what you want them to do, they should be happy that they listened to you and took your advice—whether it is to change their attitude or behavior or purchase what they are selling. This is not always the case, though.

There is a principle known as option attachment. Someone has a choice to purchase one of two puppies.

Either puppy would be a good pet for her, but each one is different. They ponder which puppy they could see themselves keeping, and no matter which one they choose, even though they are not aware of it, they worry that the other puppy will be the better of the two because the person did not choose them.

Wouldn't they feel good about the choice they made? You would think that they would be happy, relieved, or even comfortable with their decision. Yet, they are miserable. They start to question the decision that they made.

When someone is left thinking about their options too long, they tend to think that whatever they choose; they are losing something by not choosing the other thing. The initial problem is the choice they are left with. The person feels a sense of disappointment and loss when they realize that they have to let the other option go.

Persuasion research indicates that it doesn't matter if the person has personally experienced both options set in front of them, or just imagining one. Whatever option they choose, the other one becomes more attractive because they cannot have it.

The second factor of option attachment is the feeling of loss. The person felt attached to the other option when they were deliberating.

There are two ways to help counteract option attachment:

1. Don't let the person feel any sort of attachment to both of the options. You don't want them to feel a sense of loss. So, make sure that they don't have a lot of time to make the decision. Tell them that the decision has to be fast.

2. If you have to give them more than one option, make the better option more attractive to them so that they do not spend a lot of time making a decision. Don't let them feel connected with something they are never going to have. Give them info about the option and then make them understand why it is not feasible.

Chapter 25: Subliminal Persuasion

In our world, subliminal persuasion is everywhere. You can't watch television, read a magazine, or even go for a drive around town without encountering it. The definition of subliminal persuasion is the use of objects, photos, words, or another means of persuading someone into doing something or putting an idea in their head without them consciously knowing what you've done. A common example of this is advertising. When you see or hear the points made when someone is trying to sell you a product, your mind may think of the product as appealing. You usually won't know that the techniques used in the advertisement itself are the reason you feel like you need their product. Often you wouldn't have bought this item otherwise. Below is an example of how this advertising technique works.

Picture this:

A glass of soda is displayed in front of you, surrounded by warm colors. It is perfectly carbonated, as there is an emphasis on the infinite bubbles working their way to the top of the bottle. As it is being opened, the sound of carbon being released rushes from the bottle. It is a perfect day without a cloud in sight, and golden rays of the sun are shining overhead. The glare of the sun is shining on the pristine glasswork. The drink is so cold in contrast with the warm day that precipitation has formed into fat drops of water that are slowly sliding down the glass and following the way it's perfectly shaped to fit a hand.

As a model brings the drink to their lips, just a drop escapes and slides down her chin and it catches the golden light of the sun as it falls slowly out of the frame. The model's eyes slide closed slowly with pure bliss and satisfaction. The camera zeros in on the muscles of her neck contracting and stretching; and as she puts the drink down, a smile forms on her face.

You might not be in a warm area, nor may you particularly want a soda right now. However, that description was followed by your mind and you may feel thirstier than before you read it. This is because my words used subliminal persuasion to make you want the soda that was described. You've seen advertisements like this many times, and they might have worked. Never does a cold drink display so much precipitation as it does on the picture of an advertisement unless it has been sitting in water. However, because the body craves liquid when we are even a little dehydrated, the look will appeal to that natural desire. Even if what your body wants is water, this advertisement will appeal because of the unrealistic water droplets that have formed on the can or bottle.

When using this tactic in the form of manipulating another person, there are a few different ways to go about it. For instance, if you create a sense of "we" and equality in the request, it feels more inclusive. When sales clerks and advertisers work, they often create the idea that the product benefits both them and you as a consumer. They speak as if by buying their product, you not only get the benefit of having the product they think you need, but they will be happier for it.

If you word the request in a form that appeals to both you and the other person, you're more likely to achieve your goal. This form of persuasion can also combine well with cold reading techniques, as both involve the other person believing something without you outright offering the information to them.

Another form of persuasion is gathering favors. Debt is a constant in this world, and it doesn't always mean money. If you've done something for the other person recently, and have earned a form of gratitude, they're likely to feel indebted to you and therefore, more obligated to carry out your request. For example, if you save this person from an embarrassing situation, such as lending them a jacket when they've spilled a drink down their shirt, you may request a favor in return later on. Because you displayed kindness for no apparent reason that they can see, they'll feel the need to retaliate the kindness. Favors can be as large as saving someone's life, or even as small as some good advice. Every act doesn't need to be an all-out sacrifice. In fact, it shouldn't be. If someone catches a hint of deception or ulterior motives when someone is displaying such kindness, they will feel distrustful towards you, and you will lose the relationship that you've worked towards by now.

You can use this kind of persuasion technique yourself to get people to do as you wish, provided you do so subtly.

Cold Reading

Cold reading is known to be a con artist's best friend.

It provides the illusion of mind reading and magical abilities without the use of actual supernatural power. It is often used by those who make a living through fortune-telling and psychic acts. Many people have been completely sold on the act, as it is usually performed by someone who excels in reading others, has acquired enough general knowledge, and has practiced enough to deliver a very believable performance.

However, such an act is really only a form of psychology, and you could create this act yourself if you chose to.

You would do this by creating the illusion of knowing more than you really do through the power of observation. There are different names for different techniques. How many people are present decides how you should approach it. Shotgunning, for instance, is done in a large room packed with people. This is often the choice of mediums that are creating the illusion of connecting to a passed loved one because whatever they say, there is likely to be someone who can relate to the statement. When the medium speaks a few, usually vague, phrases, such as "I am connecting to an elderly man... the name John or Jack comes to mind. Does that speak to anyone?" he or she watches for anyone who expresses recognition. The names Jack and John are very common, and many people have lost a grandfather in their time. The medium will then choose one person and watch their face carefully. This is where true psychology steps in. Reading body language is essential to keeping up the ruse, as the medium will need to narrow down the descriptions of the audience members' loved ones.

If, for example, the medium says something about a white picket fence, yet no familiarity comes to this person's face, he or she will have to change their tactic carefully. He or she might explain that he never lived within a white picket fence, but wanted to, or that another relative was also present. If the audience member agrees or seems excited, this medium will know they are getting warmer. This act is continued and even peppered by what are known as "Rainbow Ruses." These are contradictory phrases such as "He was a gentle man; however, he would occasionally display a stern side". Most people have experienced these contradictory moments in their personality; however, the word choice feels so specific that it seems as if it only applies to the supposed spirit the man or woman is referring to.

Another method of cold reading, which may be more suitable for a smaller population, is to use previous knowledge when observing someone's behavior. This method is often used in detective dramas, as the act is dramatic and exciting to watch, and the character appears intelligent and clever. It is, however, easier than it may appear, as it only takes keen observation skills. For example, if you meet a new person and notice there is graphite smudged along the side of their left hand, you will know that they are left-handed, as those who are left-hand dominant must drag their hand along the previously written words to continue writing. As a left-hander myself, I would know. This phenomenon, which has been jokingly called "The Silver Surfer Syndrome", is an unquestionable indication that this person is left-handed, and you may say so with confidence as you shake their hand. The confident statement will shock this person, and they won't think to look for physical indicators. This can be used as a fun trick to amuse others, or as a shocking factor to carry into a persuasive technique, as those who have recently been surprised don't always think every factor of a decision through.

Cold reading, as any other manipulation tactic, can be used on anyone. And it is. Many people who are studied in the ways of cold reading have used it as a career, such as psychics, fortune-tellers, and any kind of con artist. Such a complicated set-up is not necessary to add this skill to your own toolbox, as you only need your own observation and shock factor. Another example is if you see someone you may already know is a student, you could confidently exclaim that they were studying late and fell asleep on their work as you note the imprint of math work on their left ear. These subtle observations build up over time, and you may gain a reputation with that person. The more you get to know someone, the more background information you will have stored away. For example, say you have a friend named Kyle. Kyle is a single father of an adorable six-year-old girl whom he spends every moment he can. To support her, he works at a grueling desk job where he files paperwork all day long and takes rude phone calls. You know that he likes light coffee with a lot of sweeteners and that he is right-handed.

Today, Kyle arrives with a large coffee in his left hand. You two always meet up every Tuesday at around ten in the morning. Today, it's almost eleven. In the back of his car is a pink hairbrush. When he gets close enough to greet you, you smell the strong aroma of black coffee rising from his cup, and you can see his clothes are wrinkled. Without asking him, what can you deduce from his situation?

I believe that his boss kept him very late and piled on the work the night prior.

He's gotten papercuts before, however even the light touch of his coffee seems to be too much pain this time, so he was working as quickly as he could. Even so, he got home late that night and overslept the next morning. Rushing to get her to school, Kyle likely tossed his daughter's hairbrush back for her to do her best with her hair on their way to school. Due to his exhaustion, he stopped to buy a coffee much stronger than he likes it before meeting with you. Of course, there are other indicators that weren't mentioned in the example. What situations you come to find yourselves observing will vary, as will the indicators that you notice.

Conclusion

The notion that dark psychology is prevalent and that it is part of our world can be a scary thought. The Dark Triad is a term in dark psychology that can be helpful when trying to pinpoint the beginning of criminal behavior.

Narcissism exhibits these traits: egotism, grandiosity, and lack of empathy.

Machiavellianism uses a form of manipulation to betray and exploit people. Those who practice this do not practice morality or ethics.

Psychopathy is a trick to those who put their trust in these types of people. They are often charming and friendly. Yet they are ruled by impulsivity, selfishness, lack of empathy, and remorselessness.

The fact that people can be used as pawns on a chessboard makes all of us want to understand dark psychology more and to figure out what it is, and how we can save ourselves from it.

There are many ailments that hypnosis can make better or even cure. And we are not just talking about mental ailments, but physical as well. Hypnosis can be used to help cure some of the side effects that are caused by chemo and radiation in cancer patients.

We all know that there has been a lot of skepticism for this alternative medicine due to the quacks that use it as a laughingstock. However, when used correctly, thistype of medicine can do a lot better than harm because it wakes people's subconscious up to letting go of things that they are holding on to that might be causing a plethora of problems in their lives.

With this being said, all of these methods can be used for good; it is just based on their intentions and the overall outcome. Those who use manipulation tactics do not use them with the intention of helping anyone. Manipulating is changing someone's thoughts, actions, and behaviors to fit someone else's (the manipulator's agenda). There is no way to sugarcoat some of these techniques. And that is why they fall under the dark psychology umbrella, because they have been used by criminals to get what they want as well.

Because we all know that someone is going to try to make us a victim of one of these methods again, sometime in our lives, and I for one would want to be as ready as I could possibly be.

There are many examples of manipulation, mind control, and persuasion in history. Some of the most infamous examples are Charles Manson, Adolph Hitler, and Ted Bundy. When you look at Charles Manson, you are able to get a profile of someone who was able to use his words and "love" for his "family" to create a cult. He was able to take young adults and make them into murders. You need to remember that Charles Manson never actually killed anyone. He simply had the members of his "family" do this through manipulation, mind control, and persuasion.

Adolph Hitler was the same way. He started by getting people to like him through persuasion. People believed that he would be one of the greatest political leaders of all time. While he did go down in history, it is not because he was a great political leader.